DATE DUE			

WHAT IS CINÉMA VÉRITÉ?

M. Ali Issari
and
Doris A. Paul

The Scarecrow
Press, Inc. Metuchen,
N.J., & London 1979

791.4301
Is 7w
125000
may 1983

Library of Congress Cataloging in Publication Data

Issari, Mohammad Ali.
    What is cinéma vérité?

      Filmography: p.
      Bibliography: p.
      Includes indexes.
      1. Moving-pictures--Philosophy. I. Paul, Doris
Atkinson, joint author. II. Title. III. Title: Cinéma
vérité.
PN1995. I85   791. 43'01   79-20110
ISBN 0-8108-1253-3

PREFACE

For the last three decades, films have been made in cinéma vérité style, and critics have analyzed, criticized and evaluated them, philosophizing about the particular approach of each film-maker. The authors of this book have compiled the major points of view of pioneers, practitioners and critics as expressed in the literature of the languages of many nations: Russian, Spanish, Italian, German, French, Danish, Swedish, Czechoslovakian and Portuguese, as well as English.

They are deeply indebted to all whose articles have appeared in periodicals across the world during the emergence of the movement (the early years following World War II), for it is upon their expressions of opinions and reviews of films that this book has been based.

Through the juxtaposition and montage of varying points of view, an organized and systematic body of information has emerged through which the serious student of cinema may discover what cinéma vérité is, and the history of its development.

Just as the philosophy of cinéma vérité is to allow the audience to experience what it was like to be present at the actual event as it was being filmed, this book attempts to lead the reader into the presence of all those involved in the development of the movement, and to draw his or her own conclusions.

The authors have brought together practical as well as philosophical statements of experts in the field--some of whom are realists, some idealists, and some fanatics in their approach. The reader may answer according to his or her own background and logic, the question, "What is cinéma vérité?" and is invited to analyze its effect on traditional commercial films and modern-day television.

CONTENTS

Preface   iii

PART I: The Enigma of a Style

I: What is Cinéma Vérité?   3

PART II: The History of Cinéma Vérité

II: Dziga Vertov   23

III: Robert Flaherty   34

IV: Neo-Realism   41

V: Nouvelle Vague   46

VI: The Free Cinema   52

VII: Television   58

PART III: The Two Schools of Cinéma Vérité

VIII: Jean Rouch: The French School   67

IX: Richard Leacock: The American School   83

X: Differences in Approach   104

PART IV: Variations on a Theme

XI: Other Pioneers and Practitioners   115

    1.   Mario Ruspoli   115
    2.   Jacques Rozier   119

v

3. Chris Marker   121
4. Albert Maysles   124
5. William C. Jersey, Jr.   133
6. Other American Practitioners   138

PART V: Technological Developments

XII: Equipment   149

PART VI: Conclusion

XIII: The End or the Way?   171

Appendix: Selected List of Cinéma Vérité Films   179

Bibliography   186

Addendum   198

Index   199

PART I:

THE ENIGMA OF A STYLE

CHAPTER I

WHAT IS CINÉMA VÉRITÉ?

When in the late nineteenth century the Lumière brothers, Louis and Auguste, introduced the phenomenon of a quick succession of pictures that would give the illusion of movement, people were stunned. In 1895 they made their first films, which dealt with trivial subjects such as workers leaving a factory or a train coming into the station. Unwittingly, perhaps, they initiated a style in film-making for which, several decades later, John Grierson coined the term "documentary."

Moving pictures were such a novelty that for a time film-makers attempted to do nothing more challenging than to photograph events as they happened. But, as might well be expected, the novelty wore off and the art of telling stories in the movies evolved. Through the years, however, makers of both feature and documentary films have been preoccupied with the problem of how to make their films more real and believable to their audiences. Decades of experimentation in the documentary tradition have given rise to various styles of film-making such as: neo-realism, nouvelle vague, free cinema, and--with the advent of television and the development of lightweight cameras and tape recorders--cinéma vérité.

Emerging from the documentary style of film-making, cinéma vérité has been particularly influenced by television techniques and pictorial journalism. * Although this style was considered by some to be a fad, it has changed the conventional approach to documentary film-making and has, to a certain extent, infiltrated theatrical films. Its aim, proclaimed by its proponents, is to present the truth. But confusion about its basic principles is still widespread. Under the name "cinéma vérité" all kinds of films are being made,

---

*The term "pictorial journalism" is used synonymously with "cinema newsreel."

many of them totally unrelated to the philosophy attributed to this style. In fact, as one critic has said, cinéma vérité has become a very "elastic" concept with an extensive range of interpretations. James C. Lipscomb cogently observes:

> ... the term 'cinéma-vérité' has been used 'loose-ly,' particularly by European writers who now call almost any film with a camera jiggle a new experiment in cinéma-vérité. They lump together all sorts of fictional experiments, interviews and standard documentaries if the technique seems to resemble direct cinema technique. Most of these films have absolutely nothing in common except celluloid. [1]

Divergent interpretations of this style by zealots and repudiators of this movement have made cinéma vérité a highly controversial subject, to the extent that it "has been hailed by some as a great new art form, branded by others as 'still-born' or 'a lie.'"[2]

Although the cinéma vérité approach to film-making started with Dziga Vertov and his concept of Kino-Eye in 1919, it wasn't until the end of World War II that this style took on momentum. As one writer has said, it is strange that an event of such inhumanity as World War II should influence film-makers to present humanity on the screen as it is.

Neo-realism, a movement toward more "truthful" presentation of film content, started in Italy and spread across the whole of Europe. Audiences with a background of personal involvement in the horrors of war, and exposed to newsreel films that presented the realities of the conflict, had a tendency to reject any presentation of war subjects packaged in the style of the studio feature film. The authenticity of a direct cinematic approach to war subjects in time spread to those of a more general nature. Sparked by the rapid acceptance of neo-realism, similar movements sprang up in other countries.

The disillusioned young meanwhile began to rebel against the older generation and their style of film-making, crying out for new and freer ways in film aesthetics and techniques. In addition, economic conditions following the war caused severe cutbacks in all phases of studio productions, thereby encouraging independent film-makers to emerge and strike out on their own to make films on low budgets with minimum technical facilities and know-how. These and other developments in cinema paved the way for a new breed of film-makers who broke away from traditional cinema and gave birth to a style christened cinéma vérité. These film-makers vigorously preached that cinema should aim at capturing life as it is lived rather than as it is re-enacted or re-invented in the old traditional way. It was their philosophy that if cinema is to be a representation of life itself, then the film-maker must submit to the "truth" within the framework of his own approach.

Admittedly, to photograph "truth" is an illusive goal. "What is truth?" is an age-old question. Mario Ruspoli, a French film-maker and a pioneer in this style of film-making, says,

> The word 'truth' is in itself so vast and complex, so full of inner and sometimes secret contradictions and represents so fluid and yet so indivisible a concept, that it can only be compared, by analogy, to a movement of thought: when given expression at the level of speech, through the sheer impossibility of saying several things at once ... it loses part of its substance. If we split the word 'truth' in order to obtain 'truths,' it loses its simultaneity. It can only be given concrete form in a broad, social and collective sense, at the level of a group, a community or a nation. 3

Applying his theory to seeking truth through cinematography, he says, "Hence the human eye, like the glass eye of his camera, is unable to capture truth in its absolute sense. It can only capture aspects, certain instants, but not the component parts in all their simultaneity."

Renato May has said that an infinite number of possible points of view exist around a subject to be photographed. Who can say "what is the true point of view, since evidently, if it exists, all the others represent only a partial vision of reality, and therefore a less true one?"4

Lucien Goldman faces up to the complexity of "truth" when he writes:

> The understanding of truth, realism, coherence and aesthetic unity today is not a simple matter of

good faith, effort, talent, or even individual genius. It is primarily a problem of the difficulties and the limits that a cultural sphere imposes on the understanding of the mind. [5]

And so go the divergent opinions about "truth" in cinema. One has to admit that "truth" must be defined by each individual within himself as well as within the context of his culture and experience. To the exponents of cinéma vérité, however, "truth" is interpreted as meaning that part of reality which is captured by the film-maker at the time he or she is making the film.

The term "cinéma vérité" was brought into the limelight by the media to describe Chronique d'un Eté ("Summer Story"), a film made by Jean Rouch and Edgar Morin, two French film-makers, which was released in Paris in 1962.

Georges Saudol, the famous French cinema historian who for the first time translated "Kino-Pravda" as "cinéma vérité" in his History of an Art: Cinema, [6] claims that Jean Rouch chose the term "cinéma vérité" to describe the style of Chronique d'un Eté as a tribute to the Soviet theorist Dziga Vertov. In 1922, Vertov introduced his theory of Cine-Eye and produced a series of newsreels called "Kino-Pravda," the equivalent of "cinéma vérité" in the Russian language.

Although Dziga Vertov used "Kino-Pravda" as a title for his series of newsreels, the term "cinéma vérité" is found in his notebooks:

Cinema can ... take the mask from the face, play a game without frolic, tell the true story with Cinéma Vérité. [7]

The use of the term, however, spread like wildfire and covered diverse approaches to film-making, thereby causing great controversy. Peter Graham comments:

... The journalists, avid for new catch-phrases, began to extend its meaning to include film-makers as different from Rouch as Drew and Leacock, Reichenbach, Marker and even Flaherty--who was claimed at the 1962 Tours short-film festival as the father of the movement.... Everyone felt comfortable in their [sic] judgments of the movement, for everyone had a different conception of it. [8]

The movement, furthermore, acquired different names from its founders, practitioners and critics in accordance with their approach and understanding of the style. To Jean Rouch and Edgar Morin it was cinéma vérité; Richard Leacock called it "living camera"; Mario Ruspoli, the Maysles brothers, and Louis Marcorelles were among those who favored "direct cinema." William Bleum designated the style as "mobile camera" but William Jersey selected the term "realistic cinema." Italians named it "film inquiry." To Armondo Plebe it became "synchronous cinema"; to Colin Young, "cinema of common sense"; to Jean-Claude Bringuier, "cinema of behavior"; to Norman Swallow, "personal documentary" or "tele-verite." Others dubbed it "film journalism," "truth film," "direct shooting," "candid-eye," and "free cinema."[*]

In spite of the variety, the term "cinéma vérité" stuck! As one writer has said, a rose by any other name still smells sweeter in French.

In March, 1963, almost a year after cinéma vérité was christened in Paris, the Radio Television Française (the French radio-television organization) invited a number of film-makers and technicians concerned with the movement to attend a cinéma vérité conference in Lyon. Leading proponents of the movement who attended the sessions included Jean Rouch, Mario Ruspoli and Edgar Morin from France; Robert Drew, Richard Leacock and Albert and David Maysles from the United States; and Michel Brault from Canada. One reporter commented on the fact that although Rossellini and Zavattini, eminent among the founders of neo-realism, Lindsay Anderson and Carl Reisz, sometimes referred to as the prophets of free cinema, and Jean-Luc Godard of the nouvelle vague movement in France were all invited, they failed to attend.

Among prominent technical men present were the Frenchman Andre Coutant, deviser of the lightweight camera Eclair, and the Swiss engineer Kudelski, the man behind the Nagra tape recorder. Their presence was significant, as without their equipment, cinéma vérité might never have "gotten off the ground." Ruspoli wrote that (because of the availability in the late 1950's of more advanced equipment which was utilized by cinéma vérité film-makers), "For the

---

[*]The three terms that have proven most hardy are the first three mentioned: cinéma vérité, living camera, and direct cinema. In this book they are used interchangeably.

first time in France, sound and picture 'stroll along' arm-in-arm with the characters in motion."[9]

It was at Lyon that the conflict between the two rival practitioners of cinéma vérité, Rouch and Leacock, came bitterly into the open. Louis Marcorelles reported that "a climate of quiet madness reigned during the course of these meetings (which were, nevertheless, respectable)."[10]

Even after its confirmation at the Lyon conference, cinéma vérité remained the subject of sharp controversy. Since it meant different things to different people, the critics were divided into two camps--the one zealously proclaiming cinéma vérité the true art form in cinema, the other side dogmatically branding it as a fallacy, anti-art, and anti-audience. Film-makers were similarly divided and critical of each other, although all of them claimed to worship at the same shrine--that of presenting the truth.

Few controversies in cinema have produced such violent clashes as those having to do with cinéma vérité. Underderstandably, this confusion creates some difficulty when one attempts to organize the varying opinions and approaches into a coherent and meaningful pattern. The following statements by prominent individuals in the medium of cinema reflect the scope and intensity of the variety of positions:

PATRICIA JAFFE

> CINEMA VERITE, or DIRECT CINEMA, is one of the most revolutionary developments in recent film history. [11]

ROY ARMES

> Cinéma-Vérité is in effect a rejection of the whole aesthetic on which the art of the cinema is based. An interesting visual style and strikingly beautiful effects are rejected as a hindrance to the portrayal of the vital truth. [12]

GEORGES SADOUL

> The camera-eye, derived in one aspect from television can by now not only transmit but fix on the screen the aesthetic impression of an event in the very instant that it is produced. Tomorrow it will

be used not only by the followers of Dziga Vertov,
the wizard film-makers like Leacock or Rouch, but
also by the thaumaturge actors, * the supporters of
the arrangement of scenes along the line of the
system of stylization used by Eisenstein in 'Ivan the
Terrible.'[13]

CHARLES FORD

It is the biggest hoax of the century. Nothing is
more fabricated, more prepared, more licked into
shape, than the so-called improvisation of cinéma
vérité. The cinéma-vérité films do not even belong
to television but more often rather to radio. The
image is absolutely superfluous, the whole technique
is bound up in radio reporting.[14]

ANDRE LABARTHE

It is one of the newest spectacles that cinema has
given us in the last ten years. Those people (i.e.,
the ones who condemn cinéma vérité) have fixed
once and for all the cinema within certain limits.
They have a prior idea about it and based on this
they judge and condemn. They don't say--This film
is good, therefore it is cinema:--but just the contrary. The duty of the critic is vice versa, to
discover where cinema renews itself and to awake
the reader's understanding of its most authentic
manifestations.[15]

MICHELANGELO ANTONIONI

The camera peeking through the key-hole is a gos-
siping eye that records what it can. And the rest
of it? Whatever goes on beyond the view from the
key-hole? It is not enough. Make ten, one hundred, two hundred holes with as many cameras
peeking through and taking miles of film. What
have you got? A mountain of material where not
only the essential aspects of an event (happening)
are caught but also the marginal or ridiculous and

---

*The thaumaturge actor, according to Eisenstein, is one who
transmits his sentiments and the material of his thoughts to
the spectator at the same moment that he experiences them.

the absurd ones. Your task will be to reduce, to select.... Besides, Pudovkin's experiments are really too well known. He used to change the meaning of certain close-ups by changing around the order of the montage. A smiling man looking at a bowl of minestrone is a gourmand; if he is looking at a dead woman with that same smile he is a cynic. So why the key-holes, the two hundred cameras and the mountain of material?[16]

ROBERT DREW

We are trying to create a filmed journalism which doesn't depend solely on the intellect, or the word, but rather in which the most important quality is cinematic. [17]

ROBERTO ROSSELLINI

The principle of cinéma-vérité is unacceptable. I believe that this method can be interesting for someone who wishes to collect scientific documentation but it is not enough from which to make a work of art. To do this you must follow the rules. If you are going to be a cyclist you have to know how to pedal. [18]

HUBERT SMITH

A cinéma-vérité film is a film that always minimizes the limitations that film imposes in transferring reality. It is a film that gets as close as possible to the visual, aural and kinesthetic sense of actual presence. And, it is a film that while compressing, rearranging, and juxtaposing the bits and pieces of reality, adheres to the truth of the story. [19]

NAZARENO FABBRETTI

Ninety percent of direct shooting is retouched, reconstructed and therefore modified as much as is necessary because, not only does the truth conceal itself more than ever, but even that very same reality. The characters who accept to play themselves in front of the camera are the first modifiers of themselves and of their own truth, inasmuch as they cease to be the virgin material of a representation or of a thesis. They never reach the felicity of the recitation of a great actor when he comes in contact with reality in the most calculated and refined of scenic fiction. [20]

JEAN ROUCH

Cinéma-vérité means that we have wanted to eliminate fiction and get closer to real life. We know that we must only pose the problem of truth, to arouse questions in the spectator. [21]

GUIDO ARISTARCO

Such a method that means beginning with the documentary in order to confer truth to the subject, begins with a dubious if not erroneous presupposition because you have to let people live their lives in front of the camera and not look at them too long through the lens, otherwise you end up by not understanding anything. [22]

CESARE ZAVATTINI

You have to give a real first and last name to a person. The man in the street caught in his day-to-day rounds must be the new hero of the cinema. [23]

PETER GRAHAM

The term cinéma vérité, by postulating some absolute truth, is only a monumental red herring. The sooner it is buried and forgotten, the better. [24]

WILLARD VAN DYKE

... it is fair to say that it is an attempt to get at the truth of a situation without straining it through a dramatist's eyes or a director's eyes or anything except that direct experience of the camera with the subject material. [25]

RAYMOND BORDE

'Cinéma-vérité' is more than a want, since it exists, and less than a theory, since it is searching for one.

These films are recorded as clinical observations and are destined for commercial exploitation.

These people are film-makers and they know it, but to assure authenticity they also make anti-films and anti-cinema. [26]

RICHARD LEACOCK

The closest I can come to an accurate definition is that the finished film--photographed and edited by the same film-maker--is an aspect of the film-maker's perception of what happened. This is assuming that he does no directing. No interference. In a funny sort of way, our films are the audience. A recorded audience. The films are a means of sharing my audience experience. [27]

HENRY BREITROSE

Cinéma-vérité, in its various manifestations, seems to be an attempt to get at the nitty-gritty of the world by observing people in the process of some crucial interactions with each other.

What seems to have happened is that important technological advances in film-making have become, for some, a magic key to the truth of the world. All of the nonsense about the film-maker, armed with camera and recorder, being able to exercise a passive 'Christlike vision' and find the real nature of the world appears to be a suitably elaborate rationale for the fact that some of the films made in this style cannot do justice to their subjects. Objectivity, in film, remains as big a myth as it ever was. [28]

JAMES BLUE

Whether people are for it or reject it entirely, Cinéma-Vérité's effect has been to force a redefinition or clarification of film aesthetics. As the coming of photography made conventional portraiture intolerable in painting, so Cinéma-Vérité

has made the conventional 'realistic style' in the
fiction film a thing of the past for many new film
makers. [29]

These sharply divergent and contradictory statements
may well make one wonder what, after all, cinéma vérité
really is. The following pages will attempt to answer this
question.

In theatrical cinema the scriptwriter's concept of reality, affected by his experience and background, are visualized
by the director, the cinematographer, and the actors. The
final product of this process, although it may be highly satisfactory from an artistic and dramatic point of view, is, more
often than not, far removed from the reality of the society
portrayed. In documentaries, the film-maker captures or
restages real events and experiences and, through organizing
these materials into a coherent form, presents his concept of
reality to the audience.

But the cinéma vérité film-maker believes that pure
cinema is the observing, recording, and presenting of reality
without controlling, staging and reorganizing it. Zavattini,
who proposed to "reduce the distance between life and performance to nothing" in his film inquiry technique, holds that
the cinema "only affirms its moral responsibility when it approaches reality in this way. The moral, like the artistic,
problem lies in being able to observe reality, not to extract
fiction from it."[30] Unlike producers of theatrical films,
cinéma vérité film-makers are not interested in entertaining,
nor do they try to teach, inform, influence, or show, as
is the case with the makers of documentary films; their
underlying motive is to convey the truth as they observe it,
rather than merely to present the facts. "The logical argument of Cinéma Vérité is that film, after all, does record
reality, and the 'aesthetic distance' of the theater is of no
corollary consideration."[31]

Peter Cowie sums up the whole thing rather well when
he writes:

> It [cinéma vérité] rejected the old style [docu-
> mentary]: action that was carefully scripted and
> scrupulously staged, the tenuous linking of widely
> disparate materials, weighty or 'witty' commen-
> taries that bludgeoned the viewer with a mass of
> facts and information. Instead, deriving its inspi-

ration from the work of Dziga Vertov and Flaherty, it relied upon bare filmed records of factual situations and events; it stressed fluidity, alertness to the unexpected, and to the subtle details of human behavior. [32]

To some cinéma vérité practitioners, extracting and presenting the truth forbids any intervention whatsoever from the film-maker; to others, certain intrusions are necessary to achieve the desired end. To some, the camera is a stimulant that brings out the truth; to others, the camera has only one right: that of recording the event. Whatever the approach in capturing truth on film, the limitations are obvious and hardly need to be rehearsed. The film-maker can cover only a small segment of all that is happening in the vicinity at a given moment--that which to him or her seems most important.

The cinéma vérité film-maker seeks to avoid judgments and subjectivity; believes in a totally objective approach. However, some critics point out that the moment the cameraman selects a shot, a subjective choice has been made, and the process of editing necessitates further subjectivity. James Lipscomb, refuting this, has said, "Probably no cinéma vérité film makers ... think that they are totally objective, and those critics who enjoy blasting at the impossibility of complete objectivity are bravely destroying strawmen."[33]

Cinéma vérité seeks to catch spontaneously the essence of what happens in reality, to photograph people living their true lives, behaving naturally and speaking their own thoughts without the interference of the film-maker. The film-maker's efforts go mainly into revealing what are to him the most essential parts of existing reality, rather than creating a new reality for the camera. He wants to present the truth as he sees it. James Blue puts it this way:

> ... In the lexicon of Cinéma Vérité, Creation as the artist's duty has been replaced by Revelation, Believability by Authenticity, Beauty by Honesty, and Preconception, in the making of the film, by Attentive Submission to the subject. The classical documentarist is drummed out for having 'used' life for the dissemination of a 'selfish point of view.' The fiction film-maker is castigated for his suspicious theatrical artifice. Because film is a photographic medium, its only proper material is be-

lieved to be life itself--not as it is recreated, but as it happens. To these men, all else is heresy. [34]

Cinéma vérité to its practitioners is a process of dis-covery--discovery of the truth. Film-makers grouped within this movement dispense with all those elements which may distort "truth." As one critic states, they are anti-fiction, anti-scenario, anti-actors, anti-studios and opposed to all the other impedimenta of conventional film-making. They make films of real people in ordinary life situations, their only means being lightweight 16mm cameras and tape recorders. No direction is permitted in this style because the film-maker is interested only in the event as it actually happens. In true cinéma vérité filming, there is no formal plot, no preconceived dialogue, and, with few exceptions, no questions are either posed or answered by the film-maker.

In referring to Richard Leacock's feeling on the matter, Louis Marcorelles writes:

> [Richard Leacock] retained his disgust for every-thing artificial, conventional, affected in the Holly-wood fashion: painted stars, Babylonian decors, celestial lighting, starlets doing their numbers. A real man does not live or act like an actor in a Hollywood film. [35]

The cinéma vérité film crew's task, therefore, is con-fined to following the subject and photographing it at its mo-ments of personal drama. The decision concerning action in each shot in effect rests with the person being photographed; the choice of whether to photograph it rests with the camera-man. Because of this unique vantage point, it is the camera-man who becomes the most important person in the crew. Generally speaking, unless the director is operating the cam-era himself, his function will be of lesser importance. It is for this reason that Jean Rouch expresses his desire to be his own cameraman, as will be discussed in a later chapter. Roy Armes says:

> The vital role of the cameraman-photographer in the Cinéma-Vérité type of ... film is indicated by the fact that Chris Marker named his photographer, Pierre Lhomme, as co-director of 'Le Joli Mai.'[36]

Marker was willing to share responsibilities in the making of the film with Lhomme because of the latter's in-

credible ability in the field as well as the fact that the cinematographer's role in a cinéma vérité film is of primary importance. (Mario Ruspoli says of Pierre Lhomme, "It is
completely staggering to see what he can extract from a take,
the way in which he continually sculpts his characters, moving
from one to another, drawing near and shifting away, forever
selecting different angles, following each gesture, 'spotting'
an expression here and there.... Whereas clumsy operators
turn out mounds of wasted film, the proportion of Lhomme's
film which the cutter cannot use is infinitesimal."[37])

Many practitioners of cinéma vérité have abolished the
words "director" and "cameraman" and substituted for them
the term "film-maker." Leacock states:

> ... there will be no such thing as a cameraman;
> there'll be film-makers. There'll be no such thing
> as editors, there'll be film-makers. It'll become
> an integrated process.[38]

In this style of film-making, where what one photographs and records is determined entirely by what is happening and by the agility of the cameraman and recordist to keep
pace with it, the editing becomes a logical progression of the
shooting. As the cameraman selects an image, the very act
of selecting reveals a point of view. Then, during the process of editing, he shows what points are most meaningful to
him. For this reason, the cameraman must be directly responsible for the editing, or closely involved with it.

The editing, however, must remain faithful to the actual event--its continuity, its character and atmosphere. The
material must be allowed to unfold itself rather than be forced
into a mold, so that the viewer can feel what the film-maker
experienced when photographing the event. Some critics believe that many of the films made by Drew, a pioneer in
cinéma-vérité, "were flawed by pushing the material into a
mold where none existed."[39] Patricia Jaffe, a New York
film editor who has worked on both documentary and theatrical
films, explains the editing of cinéma vérité films as follows:

> ... People are doing something or talking in the
> ordinary, disjointed, inarticulate way. Then ... a
> movement bursts upon the screen so true, so real
> that it is greater than any theatrical re-creation
> could ever be. It is these moments that make di-
> rect cinema so powerful a medium. The big ques-

tion then is how to sort them out and to reserve this initial excitement for the viewer. It is my firm conviction that the answer lies in allowing the viewer to experience what the film maker felt in the screening room. In other words, it is absolutely necessary that the audience experience enough of the footage to feel the rhythm of conversation or action that led to an emotionally loaded moment.... In terms of editing, this often means cutting sequences very close to the way they were shot. [40]

Ronald Kelly, who has made a number of films for the Canadian Broadcasting Company, says, "A new way of shooting needs a new way of editing."[41] He feels that a series of long continuous shots is preferable over many short shots, because this is the way life is lived.

The editing, therefore, must be true to real life, and not the manipulation of the footage by the editor to create a new reality.

The cameraman usually photographs thousands of feet of film so that in editing an optimum choice is available for selecting the material most appropriate to the unfolding progression of the subject matter. This is why cinéma vérité films are often a very expensive undertaking.

In a style that aims at an accurate representation of the event as it happened, use of explanatory narration as used in documentary films detracts from the impact of the reality presented. The main purpose of cinéma vérité films, as was discussed previously, is to make the viewer an observer of the drama as it unfolds and is recorded by the film-maker. Therefore, to bring an intermediator between the event and the viewer is against the philosophy of this style. Nevertheless, these films sometimes utilize narration as a bridge to cover gaps in the story line or to explain the footage itself. In other words, narration is used to pick up things the film-maker missed with his camera. Ideally, however, a cinéma vérité film is one that can stand alone without explanatory narration.

"Structure" may be said to be the most important single element in the success of a cinéma vérité film. A film without a structure, i.e., without beginning, development, and ending, will not work out successfully. It is not enough to show bits and fragments of life--the footage must be organized coherently to follow a theme. In some instances, a theme emerges during shooting, and sometimes nothing of significance happens around which the film-maker can build a structure. For this reason, some cinéma vérité films can end up only as exercises in photography and not as total films.

The cinéma-vérité movement owes its existence primarily to the technological developments in film equipment. Mario Ruspoli has said, "Technique having become 'second nature,' the cameraman with an alert ear could in a sense 'live' the filmed episode and directly participate in it."[42] Another writer comments, "Such equipment comes close to the hypothetical 'camera pen' envisioned by the French film-maker and critic, Alexandre Astruc, with which one could 'write' films as directly as one writes on paper."[43]

Because of the technological developments in film equipment, film-makers were able to use their tools of trade, the camera and tape recorder, to express themselves more freely--like a painter with his brush or a writer with his pen. And with the advent of cinéma vérité, film-makers, now mobile with lightweight equipment and faster film stocks, entered this new field of experimentation in the art of cinema.

Varied approaches to cinéma vérité have formed a wide spectrum which may generally be divided into two distinctive schools. One has included in large part the American film-makers and the other, French film-makers, represented in the main by styles exercised by Richard Leacock and Jean Rouch, respectively. Among important men and movements paving the way for the emergence of cinéma vérité were Dziga Vertov and his theory of Cine-Eye; Robert Flaherty and his approach of Non-Preconception; movements such as neo-realism in Italy, nouvelle vague in France, free cinema in England and, in particular, the advent of television. Each made its distinctive mark on this new style of film-making which left a significant impact on the art and craft of filmmaking across the world.

In the following pages, some of the key proponents of the cinéma vérité philosophy and practitioners of the cinéma vérité style will be discussed, along with highlights in the progress of movements devoted to it.

NOTES

[1]James C. Lipscombe, "Correspondence and Controversy: Cinéma Vérité," Film Quarterly, XVIII, No. 2 (Winter, 1964-1965), page 62.

[2]Peter Graham, "Cinéma Vérité in France" ("Three Views on Cinema Verite"), Film Quarterly, XVII, No. 4 (Summer, 1964), page 30.

[3]Mario Ruspoli, "Towards a New Film Technique in the Developing Countries: The Light-Weight Synchronized Cinematographic Unit," report for the United Nations Educational, Scientific and Cultural Organization, Paris (September 29, 1964), (mimeographed), page 14.

[4]Renato May, "Dal Cinema al Cinéma-Véritá," Bianco e Nero, Anno XXV, Numero 4-5 (April-May, 1964), page 15 of translation.

[5]Lucien Goldman, "Cinema and Sociology; Consideration of A Summer Chronicle," Artsept 2 (April-June, 1963), page 5 of translation.

[6]Georges Sadoul, Histoire d'un Art: Le Cinéma (Paris: Flammarion, 1940).

[7]Georges Sadoul, "Actualité de Dziga Vertov," Cahiers du Cinéma, Vol. XXIV, No. 144 (Juin, 1963), page 28.

[8]Graham, loc. cit.   [9]Ruspoli, loc. cit.

[10]Louis Marcorelles, "Truth Fair," Cahiers du Cinéma, Vol. XXIV, No. 140 (February, 1963), page 27.

[11]Patricia Jaffe, "Editing Cinéma Vérité," Film Comment, III, No. 3 (Summer, 1965), page 43.

[12]Roy Armes, French Cinema since 1946, Vol. II: The Personal Style. (Amsterdam: Drukkerijen vh, Ellerman Harms NV, 1966), p. 125.

[13]Enzo Natta, "Pro e Contro il Cinéma-Vérité," Rivista del Cinematografo (November, 1963), page 418.

[14]Ibid.   [15]Ibid.

[16]Michelangelo Antonioni, "Infrarosso-La realte e il cinema-diretto," Cinema Nuovo, XIII. No. 167 (Gennaio-Febbraio, 1964), page 8.

[17]André S. Labarthe et Louis Marcorelles, "Entretien avec Robert Drew et Richard Leacock," Cahiers du Cinéma, Vol. XXIV, No. 140 (Fevrier, 1963), page 24.

[18]Natta, loc. cit.

[19]Hubert Smith, "The University Film Director and Cinéma-Vérité," Journal of the University Film Producers Association, XIX, No. 2 (1967), page 58.

[20]Natta, op. cit., page 419.

[21]Ibid., page 418.

[22]Ibid., page 419.

[23]Ibid.

[24]Graham, op. cit., page 36.

[25]Perry Miller, "Interview with Willard Van Dyke, James C. Lipscomb, and William C. Jersey, Jr.," (May 16, 1967), New York Film Council (mimeographed).

[26]Raymond Bordé, "Problèmes du Cinéma-Vérité," Positif, No. 49 (December, 1962), pages 1-3.

[27]James Blue, "One Man's Truth, An Interview with Richard Leacock," Film Comment, III, No. 2 (Spring, 1965), page 16.

[28]Henry Breitrose, "On the Search for the Nitty-Gritty: Problems and Possibilities in Cinéma-Vérité" (Three Views on Cinema Verite) Film Quarterly, XVII, No. 4 (Summer, 1964), pages 36 and 40.

[29]James Blue, "Thoughts on Cinéma Vérité and a Discussion with the Maysles Brothers," Film Comment, II, No. 4 (Fall, 1965), page 23.

[30]Cesare Zavattini, "Some Ideas on the Cinema," Sight and Sound, XXIII, No. 1 (July/September, 1953), page 65.

[31]William Bleum, Documentary in American Television (New York: Hastings House, 1965), page 125.

[32]Peter Cowie, editor, A Concise History of the Cinema, Vol. 2: Since 1940 (New York: A. S. Barnes & Co., 1971) p. 238.

[33]James C. Lipscomb, loc. cit.

[34]Blue, "Thoughts on Cinéma Vérité and a Discussion with the Maysles Brothers," loc. cit.

[35]Louis Marcorelles, "The Leacock Experiment," Cahiers du Cinéma, Vol. XXIV, No. 140 (February, 1963), page 16.

[36]Armes, op. cit., page 17.

[37]Ruspoli, op. cit., page 25.

[38]Ian A. Cameron and Mark Shivas, "Interviews," Movie, No. 8 (April, 1963), page 17 (interview with Richard Leacock).

[39]Jaffe, op. cit., page 45.

[40]Ibid.

[41]Norman Swallow, Factual Television (New York: Hastings House, Communication Arts Books, 1966), page 201.

[42]Mario Ruspoli, "Experiments in the Cinema and in Television: The Leger Synchronous Group," Filmselezione, No. 19-20, translation, page 6.

[43]"The Technology," Film Quarterly, Vol. XVII, No. 4 (Summer, 1964), page 24 (no author indicated in source).

PART II:

THE HISTORY OF CINEMA VERITE

CHAPTER II

DZIGA VERTOV

In the Soviet Union, after the Revolution of 1917, Lenin declared cinema the most important medium for the education and instruction of the masses. In its attempt to educate the people of the republic to the Communist ideology, the government took complete control of the film industry. Great film-makers of the Soviet Union, such as Sergei Eisenstein, V. Podovkin, Kuleshov, Dovzhenko, the Vassiliev brothers and others, emerged from this period. The innovations in cinematic structure that they introduced not only advanced the Communist dogma but also startled the film world of that day. The new mode of Soviet cinema was "Socialist Realism"--an approach toward portraying real life rather than dramatic fantasy on the screen. If cinema was to be an effective tool in teaching and influencing the masses, it was necessary to convince audiences with a realistic presentation of their own image. In this pursuit the Russian film-makers started utilizing real locations instead of stage sets; peasants played the part of peasants; real workers appeared in the roles of workers, and so on.

One of these new film-makers who saw great possibilities in cinema as an effective weapon in the social struggle was Dziga Vertov (pseudonym for Denis Arkadievitch Kaufman). One gains an insight into the character of the man by considering the origin of the name he chose for himself. Dziga is derived from the Ukrainian word suggesting perpetual motion; a spinning top or constantly revolving wheel. It is also related to the word tzigana--the word for gypsy. Not satisfied with having just a first name that gave the impression of action, he chose Vertov for his last name--a word derived from the Russian verb, "vertat," which means to pivot or whirl.

Dziga Vertov, this amazing man, is considered to be

the greatest theoretician and the prophet father of the core
idea of cinéma vérité. He believed that "it was the function
of the motion picture as a proletarian art to portray the life
of the people in all its intense and intimate detail,"[1] and
wanted to banish from cinema everything not taken from real
life.

He was born in 1896, matured with the Russian Revolution, and died in 1954.[2] In his youth he was a poet and
musician, fascinated by the imagery of sound. On a primitive phonograph he recorded various sounds such as that of
the cascading waterfalls and the whirring of machinery, attempting to achieve what is now called "concrete music."
Following the October Revolution of 1917 he moved from the
medium of audio-imagery to the visual. In 1918, as a writer
for the Soviet "Film Weekly" (Kino-Nedelia), he edited and
wrote captions for the documentary films of the civil war.*
Later he became a newsreel cameraman, and from this experience developed a concept that cinema should exclude anything not taken from life itself. He wanted to make films
outside the studio, with no actors, sets, scripts or other
paraphernalia of traditional cinema.

In 1919, he issued his first manifesto, "Kinoks-Revo-
lution,"[3] in which he condemned the story film as alien to
the temper and needs of Soviet audiences, and called for a
new style of cinematographic reportage based on documenting
real life. His manifesto appeared in extended form in Lef
magazine (No. 3, 1922), presenting in greater detail the
theory of Cine-Eye. In the same year he organized "Kino-
Pravda" (cinema truth or cinéma vérité), a filmic supple-
ment to the official Russian state newspaper, Pravda. He
produced 23 issues of this film magazine. The French historian, Georges Sadoul, however, claims that Vertov's "Kino-
Pravda" was not only a slogan but that at the end of his life
his ideas of Cine-Eye had evolved into cinéma vérité in its
modern and contemporary sense. Sadoul tells us, "I was
gratified to find at least a Vertov text from 1940 in which he
uses the expression cinéma-vérité in the sense which it has
now come to mean."[4] Then, he quotes Vertov as saying:

> Cinéma Vérité is by Cine-Eye and for Cine-Eye but
> with the truth of its resources and possibilities.

---

*The reader should realize that films were still silent during
this period.

It is photographing people without make-up from angles that take them unaware, and getting them with the camera-eye at a moment when they are not acting and letting the camera strip their thoughts bare.[5]

One of the documentaries Vertov made, using his concept of "catching people unaware," was the chronicle of the life of a day in a large city, from sunrise to sunset. He used the Cine-Eye technique "as a means of making the invisible visible, the obscure clear, the hidden obvious, the disguised exposed, and acting not acting."[6]

Perhaps the best way to explain Vertov's theory of Cine-Eye is to quote at some length from his "Notebooks":

The 'Kino-Eye' is in the realm of 'that which the naked eye does not see,' a microscope and a telescope of time, an x-ray eye, the 'candid' eye, the remote control of a camera.

All these various definitions mutually complement each other; the 'Kino-Eye' includes:

All film methods;
All cinematic images;
All methods and means by which the truth can be shown.

Not the 'Kino-Eye' for its own sake, but the truth by means of the 'Kino-Eye.' Cinematic truth.[7]

On capturing the truth by means of the Cine-Eye, Vertov says:

1. If 'Kino-Pravda' is truth shown by means of the cinematic eye, then a shot of the banker will only be true if we can tear the mask from him, if behind his mask we can see the thief.

2. The only way we can divest him of his mask is by concealed observation, by concealed photography: i.e., by means of hidden cameras, supersensitive film and light sensitive lenses, infra-red film for night and evening shooting, noiseless cameras. Constant readiness of the camera for filming. Immediate shooting of a perceived object.[8]

Vertov goes on to point out that it is necessary for the camera to peer behind the mask people assume before others, because one must perceive their thoughts to know what they truly are:

> ... the hypocrite, the flatterer, bureaucrat, the spy, the bigot, the blackmailer, the contriver, etc., who hide their thoughts while playing one role or another, take their masks off only when no one can see them or hear them. To show them without their masks on--what a difficult task that is, but how rewarding. [9]

This task, however, was virtually impossible at the time Vertov expounded his theories. In the early 1920s his ideas were in the realm of prophecy, for films were still silent; the cameras were heavy and cumbersome, and the technology of film-making was still in its infancy. Vertov's significance, according to Sadoul, however, lies in his capacity to "imagine the possibilities of future technical development, which lay 40 years ahead. He was hailed as a Russian futurist, and knew, like his teacher Maïakowski (albeit in another way) how to announce and describe the future and the epoch we are now entering."[10] He was a pioneer with vision.

With the new lightweight cameras and tape recorders and fast, sensitive film, the film-maker of today can go any place virtually unnoticed and record in sight and sound that which he believes to be the decisive moment of a given situation, as Vertov envisioned in his Cine-Eye theories.

Vertov's own words are again the most effective means of explaining his method of obtaining the truth:

> I am a film writer. A cinepoet. I do not write on paper, but on film. As with every writer, I have to make work notes. Observations. Not on paper, however, but on film. Together with longer poems, I write short novels, sketches, verse.... I can only write simultaneously, as the events are occurring.... I do not demand that the cameraman be at the scene of a fire two hours before it breaks out. But I cannot permit that he go to film a fire a week after the fire has gone out.... [11]

Vertov's method of capturing the true moments of life itself was simply to go everywhere with his camera. In a state of near-euphoria (although what he envisioned was impossible to achieve in his time) he wrote:

> I am mechanical and today I am breaking free
> from human immobility. I am in continuous move-
> ment, I come up close to things, I withdraw from
> them, I nip in and out among them, I perch on top
> of them, I am near the horse's nose when he is
> galloping, I plunge into the midst of a crowd, I am
> running in front of charging soldiers, I can turn
> over on my back, I can fly with aeroplanes. [12]

Discussing the Cine-Eye, Paul Rotha writes in his book, The Film Till Now,

> ... The roving lens of the camera has the power of
> the human eye. It can and does go everywhere and
> into everything. It climbs the side of a building
> and goes in through the window; it travels over fac-
> tories, along steel girders, across the road, in and
> out of trains, up a chimney stack, through a park
> ... into the houses of the rich and poor; it stands
> in the street, whilst cars, trams, buses, carts
> flash by it on all sides ... it follows this person
> down that alley and meets that one round the cor-
> ner. [13]

With his camera, Vertov investigated every aspect of people and places that intrigued him. He hid and watched and photographed. Using the telephoto lens and crouching behind bushes, he and his cameramen filmed poignant scenes such as a family weeping at a grave. This candid camera method, which he called "Improvised Life," was elaborated primarily by his younger brother, Mikhail Kaufman. They photographed people unaware, sometimes by telephoto lens and sometimes by selecting people sufficiently absorbed in what they were doing to forget the presence of the camera. This concept of attempting to photograph people who are so deeply involved in their task as to forget the presence of the camera forms part of the approach taken by the American cinéma vérité film-makers, and in particular by Richard Leacock.

To Vertov, the photography of incidents of everyday life was not in itself cinematic truth. He stressed the principle and importance of montage "to combine science with cinematic depiction in the struggle to reveal truth ... to decipher reality."[14] He wrote:

Kino-eye is:

montage, when I select a theme (to pick a theme
among a possible thousand);

montage, when I keep watch over the execution of
the theme (of a thousand observations, to make a
proper choice);

montage, when I establish the order of exposition
of what has been shot according to the theme (of a
thousand possible combinations to select the most
adequate, basing one's self as much upon the qualities of the filmed documents as upon the requirements of the chosen theme). [15]

Vertov came to realize that it was not enough "to show
bits of truth on the screen, separate frames of truth." Rather, "these frames must be thematically organized so that the
whole is also truth."[16]

He believed that the organization of photographed truth,
the presentation of it as a whole truth, is a difficult task and
that "thousands of experiments must be conducted in order to
master this new field of cinematographic work."[17] Paul
Rotha offers this summary: "The Vertov theory, in brief,
assumes that the camera lens has the power of the moving
human eye to penetrate every detail of contemporary life and
its surroundings, to an accompaniment of sound."[18] Sadoul
enlarges on this thought further:

When Vertov spoke of the Kino-Apparat (Cine-
Camera) functioning like a Cine-Eye, he admitted
to his great theory not the camera alone, but in
addition the cutting-bench and projector, which
were, in his opinion a mechanical unity. Thus the
Cine-Eye was not a mere recording process, but
it could organize (through editing). So its recording
was by no means passive. [19]

Therefore, according to Vertov's theories, cinéma
vérité could also be made by splicing together pre-existing
films so long as these were based on the actual or on the
documentary, a concept rejected by the cinéma-vérité practitioners in later years. Vertov believed in researching the
content of his film thoroughly before editing it. This enabled
him to achieve the purest possible essence of truth on the

subject through the editing process. It is interesting to note that Robert Flaherty, who was pioneering a new kind of film-making in the United States at this time, also believed in knowing the subject thoroughly, but in his case, as a prerequisite to the actual shooting rather than during the editing process.

In other words, Vertov, because of the nature of his profession as an editor of newsreel footage (already photographed material), had to extract the truth during the editing process, while Flaherty studied his subjects thoroughly to gain a complete insight before photographing them. Many cinéma vérité exponents take exception to Flaherty's approach, believing that first impressions of a subject are most important and would be sacrificed if the film-maker did advance research. But the purpose of each must be borne in mind: Vertov's intent was to present a predetermined idea to the public; Flaherty's was to record a naturalist document; and the cinéma vérité exponents mean to capture life as they see it.

As early as 1923, Vertov insisted that Cine-Radio, or sound editing, should also become an important aspect of film-making. From the beginning (as has been stated before) he had been fascinated with documenting sound. He named his idea of combining Cine-Eye and Cine-Radio (Radio-Ear) "Living Camera," a term adopted by some American film-makers many years later. He said, "Radio-Eye, Cine-Eye and Radio-Ear are all methods of organizing how we see and hear the whole world, and they enable working people of all lands to see, to hear, and to understand themselves and each other in a systematic way."[20]

The techniques of the living camera proposed by Vertov have influenced many American and European film-makers such as Leacock, Maysles, Rouch and Ruspoli, who are among the pioneers in the cinéma vérité movement.

In addition to montage, Vertov used all other cinematic devices available to him at the time to present his truth--slow motion, fast motion, reversed motion, still photography, split screen, etc.--techniques which cinéma vérité practitioners consider artificial and untrue. All such devices were used in his last silent film, The Man with the Movie Camera.

One of Vertov's favorite methods was cross-cutting,

placing in close sequence shots from one city to another, even from one country to another. He said:

> I am the Cinema-Eye. I make a man more
> perfect than Adam. I take the strongest and most
> skillful arms from one man, from another I take
> the fastest and nimblest legs. From a third I take
> the most handsome and expressive head. With film
> editing I create a new man, and a perfect one. [21]

Paul Rotha says that perhaps Vertov was "over-fond of cross-cutting.... From streets being washed to a girl washing herself ... from the soft beds of the rich to the hard benches in the park.... He was over-inclined to flash a series of one-foot shots before the audience and blind them."[22]

Although Vertov's use of cinematic devices and montage would be utterly unacceptable to current cinéma vérité practitioners, he never used them as an end in themselves, but as one more means of reaching "the truth" that he was seeking. He maintained that "the important thing is not [to] separate form from content. The secret lies in unity of form and content."[23]

In summing up his theory of Cine-Eye at a lecture he delivered in Paris in 1929, Vertov remarked: "The history of Kino-Eye has been a relentless struggle to modify the course of world cinema, to place in cinematic production a new emphasis of the 'unplayed' film over the played film, to substitute the document for the mise-en-scène to break out of the proscenium of the theater and to enter the arena of life itself."[24] John Howard Lawson, however, says: "This sweeping generalization is in itself an abstraction, failing to take account of the fact that the cinematic document is itself a mise-en-scène, a selection of the material which cannot encompass the whole 'arena of life itself.'"[25]

Vertov further believed his films to be objective documents, albeit poetic--a scientific view of society. It has been remarked, however, that it is not entirely correct to claim that Vertov depicted "reality" in the life of the Russian people: "There were contradictions and conflicts in Soviet life which were far beyond the vision of Vertov's camera-eye. What he captured in his documents was an emotion much simpler than the reality, but expressing something that was deeply felt in the lives of the people."[26]

Vertov was not able to put his theory of Kino-Eye in its entirety into practice during his lifetime because of the lack of proper equipment and the resistance his ideas received from a group of theatrical people who called themselves "The Factory of the Eccentric Actor." These people believed that cinema art should move toward the traditional and controlled acting of the theater rather than toward the "reality" preached by Vertov. Their ideas, however, soon died out and Vertov's endured. It was only some 40 years after his manifesto of Cine-Eye that equipment came on the market to make his theories workable. As Rotha comments, "Vertov in practice ran away from Vertov in theory."[27] But Vertov's importance grew with the years because he had prophesied the cinematic future. Many of his theories were reshuffled and adopted in the late 1950s by film-makers in Europe and the United States who benefited from important technological breakthroughs which were decisive factors in bringing about cinéma vérité.

Vertov might be called the father of cinéma vérité, as his farsighted theories paved the way for the emergence of a new style that would influence the entire spectrum of film-making. His primary significance lay not only in his ability to foresee technical and cinematic developments in the future, but also in his courage to manifest his ideas and direct the attention of future film-makers toward a more realistic treatment of the film aesthetic. His theories, no doubt, conceptualized the core idea of the cinéma vérité movement and greatly influenced the approach to documentary film-making.

NOTES

[1]John Howard Lawson, Film, the Creative Process (second edition), (New York: Hill and Wang, 1964), page 73.

[2]For bio-filmography of Dziga Vertov, refer to Georges Sadoul, "Bio-Filmographie de Dziga Vertov," Cahiers du Cinéma, No. 146 (Août, 1963), pp. 21-29.

[3]In Russian, Kinoki Perevorot. Kinok was made from the combination of the Russian word Kino (cinema) and Oko (eye), to describe a group of young enthusiasts originally called "Soviet Tronkh," or "Council of Three," centered

around Dziga Vertov. Georges Sadoul, "Actualité de Dziga Vertov," Cahiers du Cinéma, Vol. XXIV, No. 144 (Juin, 1963), page 23.

[4]Georges Sadoul, "Dziga Vertov," Artsept No. 2. Le Cinéma et la Vérité (Avril/Juin, 1963), page 19.

[5]Dziga Vertov, "Fragments," Artsept No. 2. Le Cinéma et la Vérité (Avril/Juin, 1963), page 20.

[6]Dziga Vertov, "The Writings of Dziga Vertov," Film Culture, No. 25 (Summer, 1962), page 55. ("From the Notebooks of Dziga Vertov.")

[7]Ibid., page 54.

[8]Ibid., page 57.

[9]Ibid.

[10]Georges Sadoul, "Actualité de Dziga Vertov," op. cit., page 24.

[11]Vertov, "The Writings of Dziga Vertov," op. cit., page 58.

[12]Sadoul, "Dziga Vertov Newsreel," op. cit., page 25.

[13]Paul Rotha and Richard Griffith. The Film Till Now, a Survey of World Cinema (London: Spring Books, 1967), page 224.

[14]Vertov, op. cit., page 55.

[15]Ibid., page 65.

[16]Ibid., page 55.

[17]Ibid.

[18]Rotha, op. cit., pages 122-123.

[19]Sadoul, "Actualité de Dziga Vertov," op. cit., page 26.

[20]Dziga Vertov, "Fragments," op. cit., page 19.

[21]Sadoul, "Dziga Vertov Newsreel," op. cit., page 22.

[22]Rotha, op. cit., page 246.

[23]Vertov, "The Writings of Dziga Vertov," op. cit., page 56.

[24]Ibid., page 58 ("Dziga Vertov on Kino-Eye, Lecture I").

[25]Lawson, op. cit., page 112.

[26]Ibid., page 86.

[27]Rotha, loc. cit.

CHAPTER III

ROBERT FLAHERTY

A contemporary of Dziga Vertov was an American, Robert Flaherty (1884-1951), a professional explorer working as a prospector for mining concerns in North America. As a means of making notes on his explorations in the Hudson Bay area he took a motion picture camera with him for the first time in 1916, at the suggestion of his employer, Sir William MacKenzie. Flaherty's interest in the medium of cinema was thereby aroused. In particular, he became fascinated with recording the native life of the Eskimos with whom he had spent many years. The outcome was Nanook of the North (1922), a film which shows Flaherty's deep feeling for the Eskimos and their environment.

Flaherty's Nanook was perhaps the first film made on cinéma vérité principles by an American film-maker--without actors, studio, story, or stars--with just everyday people doing everyday things, being themselves. This film, in spite of many of its kind that have succeeded it, is still being shown and admired all over the world.

One reason for the film's general acclaim is probably its truthfulness: it is taken from real life and shows only real people. As Flaherty's wife Frances wrote, this was a film in which audiences were able to identify--not with film stars, but

> ... with life itself, with universal life of which we and these people are a part. When Nanook and Nyla and little Allegoo smile out at us from the screen, so simple, so genuine and true, we, too, become simple, genuine, true. They are themselves: we, in turn, become ourselves. Everything that might separate us from these people falls away. In spite of all our differences, indeed the more be-

cause of them, we are one with these people. And
that feeling of oneness can deepen and become a
feeling of oneness with all peoples and all things. [1]

Flaherty studied Nanook thoroughly before filming him.
He shared his life and his environment, in essence becoming
a member of his family. He was not satisfied merely to
follow the Eskimo around and photograph him, as is the practice with some cinéma vérité film-makers of today. Instead,
he secured Nanook's full cooperation, to the point that in
front of the camera he ceased to be anonymous and became
his real self. Unlike the procedure followed in traditional
film-making, Flaherty first photographed the scenes he needed
and then wrote his scenario, editing his footage to fit the
story. However, all through the process he made sure that
nothing artificial entered the picture.

As Mrs. Flaherty said of her husband's approach to
the making of Nanook:

> ... let one false gesture, one least unnatural move-
> ment, the slightest hint of artificiality, appear, and
> separateness comes back. Again we are just look-
> ing at the people on the screen, and the whole ex-
> perience of identity, of oneness, of participation,
> becomes impossible, could not happen, could never
> be. The secret of Nanook lies, I believe, in those
> two words, 'Being themselves.' Not Acting, but
> Being. [2]

Since Flaherty's upbringing and experience had been
in the world's wilderness, he sought disappearing cultures in
order to make ethnographical films of primitive peoples. His
scientific record of vanishing cultures was often made more
complete through an intentional revival of past conditions and
customs. In this vein, apart from Nanook of the North,
Flaherty made Moana about the Polynesians (1926) and Man
of Aran about islanders living off the coast of Ireland (1934).

After he made Nanook Flaherty went to an entirely
different part of the world to make Moana as an extensive
ethnographic description of life in the Samoas. The betrothal
of Fa'angase to the beautiful Moana served as the central
theme in the documentary.

The everyday life of the people of these South Pacific
islands was the grist for his mill: harpoon fishing, the

preparation of vegetable fibers to make clothing, trapping of the wild boar, and cultivation of their staple food, taro. Scenes in this film are contrasted with the backdrop of the ever-present sea in all its moods: its calm and its violent storms on the coral reef.

Flaherty's Man of Aran (released in 1934) is considered by some authorities to be his masterpiece. It won admiration from famous documentarians such as Paul Rotha and many others. The film is a "hymn to the unremitting toil of a handful of men and women, clinging to a small isolated rocky island, threatened by the angry sea, off the coast of Western Ireland,"[3] writes Luc de Heusch in his Survey of Ethnographic and Sociological Films. The main characters in Man of Aran are Michael, a young fisherman, his father, also a fisherman and shark hunter, and Michael's mother.

Flaherty filmed scenes of the father breaking stones to prepare a potato field, mending his boat and hunting shark; the mother gathering seaweed, searching for arable soil in the cracks of the rock to carry in a basket to the field. Michael assists his mother. The rigors of hunting shark in a violent sea, and the final destruction of the boat, tossed by waves and shattered on the beach, graphically illustrate the constant struggle for mere survival on Aran.

Flaherty spent two years on the Aran islands to produce this faithful description of a hostile environment and a courageous people. "What emerged was a film of far greater professional polish than Nanook of the North or Moana, and with epic grandeur."[4] In 1934 he made Tabu with F. W. Murnau; in 1937, Elephant Boy with Zoltan Korda; and in 1948, he made Louisiana Story.

In all his films he used actual people in their natural locations. He lived among the people he intended to photograph until he discovered the distinctive drama of their existence. In his films there is no artificial story or background and there are no fictitious people.

Despite his lack of training in cinema, Flaherty's camera was personal and informal. It used the imagery of a poet and created a cinematic principle based on capturing the truth of life in many ways unknown to cinema prior to his time. By adopting the language and customs of the people with whom he lived, he succeeded in being one of them and was never regarded as an intruder. He was able thereby to film the people without marring their naturalness.

> ... Flaherty intuitively sensed the limitations of the impersonal camera and the restrictions of the formal frame. By involving himself in his material, he established a cinematic principle which parallels Werner Heisenberg's uncertainty principle in physics, namely that the mere observation of nuclear (and cinematic) particles alters the properties of these particles. [5]

Flaherty's use of real-life experience and actual people in his films corresponded with the theories of Vertov, embodied the phenomena that later launched Italian neo-realism, and has become the watchword of some of the cinéma vérité practitioners. It is the opinion of certain critics, including Patricia Jaffe, that cinéma vérité can be traced back to Flaherty. She says:

> Cinéma vérité grew directly out of the Flaherty tradition. Flaherty's careful studies of culture and custom bore fruit in the devotion with which other great documentarists (Lorentz, Hurwitz, Grierson, Ivens, Meyers, Van Dyke) attempted to put reality on film. All over the world film makers took cameras on location to photograph people against their natural environment. [6]

Like his contemporary, Vertov, Flaherty in filming moved "out of the proscenium of the theater and into the arena of life itself." Vertov, however, was a theoretician writing extensively about his theories, whereas Flaherty simply made films with little written or verbal discussion of his "non-preconception" approach to recording the struggle of man against his environment. Both wanted to capture reality as they saw it, but Flaherty approached this venture as an ethnographer rather than as a journalistic social educator like Vertov. Flaherty's technique in essence was to explore, discover and then reveal what came out of life itself.

Rouch, in a round-table conference on cinéma vérité at the Tours Festival (1963), retraced the history of the movement and made an interesting comparison between the approaches of Vertov and Flaherty. "Dziga Vertov," he said, "thought the eye of the camera was a way of seeing the world, and that there existed a cinematographic reality different from what is actually seen; that is to say, he attached considerable importance to editing. "[7] Because of this approach, it was necessary for Vertov to rely on montage to achieve unity.

Rouch pointed out that Flaherty, on the other hand, relied on the "participating camera," which the people got used to and by means of which he recorded on film just what he wished to say. Whereas Vertov settled his camera and waited for something to happen, Flaherty made preparations to film what he expected to happen. Rouch illustrated his thesis by adding,

> ... We have perfect examples of this in "The Man with a Camera" ... [in which] he shows children fascinated by a magician in action. It is not the magician Vertov filmed (or rather Kaufman, since he was cameraman) but the children. On the contrary, when Flaherty shot 'Moana,' he shot thousands of feet of film to get a certain expression which he defines in an extraordinary manner as the look of a man being totally proud and scared at the same time; the man who suffers but is proud of being tattooed. [8]

Flaherty spent an immense amount of time and energy preparing for and producing his films. When making Man of Aran he waited one full year to photograph the right storm sequence. He has been criticized for not filming events as they occurred, but he knew such storms took place and simply waited until the one came along that was just right for his purposes. He was extravagant in filming events until the precise moment of truth was captured on the film. Mrs. Flaherty states that while filming Moana, "we filmed and filmed. We went mad with filming, let the camera see everything and see it exhaustively."[9] And she explains that while shooting Louisiana Story, Flaherty "brought all this [footage] to the screen, and screened and screened it, and went out and shot again, for one reason only: to give the camera a chance to find that 'moment of truth,' that flash of perception, that penetration into the heart of the matter, which he knew the camera, left to itself, could find."[10]

James Blue refers to Flaherty's principle of filming, based on "non-preconception," as an "odyssey of discovery," and adds, "Flaherty, however, once his notions were formed, went on to stage or to provoke whatever might satisfy the needs of his film, according to his own sensitivity."[11] Fla-

herty has also been criticized for this method, because once
he had established his concept of "truth" of the culture he
intended to record, he re-enacted or restaged parts of the
film. Nevertheless, his main theory in cinema was non-preconception, as against the practice of preconceiving non-
entertainment films for educational and social purposes. He
photographed things as they had happened in real life if an
opportunity did not present itself to photograph them as they
were happening--rather than making up anything that did not
come out of life itself. He revived conditions and customs
of former importance; e. g. , in Nanook the Eskimos hunt with
harpoons rather than rifles, and in Moana elaborate dances
were reconstructed from the memory of the Samoan chiefs.
These were things that had been and still could be true, and
bore no taint of fiction or artificiality. Flaherty has also
been criticized, particularly in Man of Aran, for recording
a past way of life and ignoring current serious problems such
as cruel landlords, poor housing and social inequities. However, he claimed that his films were meant to portray man's
age-old struggle to survive against the elements and not to
record the recent decadent influence of "white man's civiliza-
tion. "[12]

In short, Vertov "intruded" upon his film through
editing to get a particular idea across to his audience, whereas Flaherty manipulated his films, primarily in shooting, to
leave the fullest possible scientific record of a dying culture.
Like Vertov, Flaherty of course suffered from lack of lightweight cameras, tape recorders, and fast film, which became available to the cinéma vérité practitioners in the late
1950s. Both men, however, maintained that presenting real
life is much more valid than any artificial reproduction of it,
and both were important figures in initiating the world movement toward the presentation of "truth" in cinema. So it
may be safe to assume that cinéma vérité grew directly out
of the traditions of Vertov and Flaherty, two contemporary
film-makers, one in the Soviet Union and one in America.

NOTES

[1]Frances Hubbard Flaherty, The Odyssey of a Film-
Maker, Robert Flaherty's Story (Urbana, Illinois: Beta Phi
Mu, 1960), pages 17-18.

[2]Ibid.

[3]Luc de Heusch, "The Cinema and Social Science: A Survey of Ethnographic and Sociological Films," United Nations Educational, Scientific and Cultural Organization, No. 16, 1962, page 38.

[4]Erik Barnouw, Documentary, A History of the Non-Fiction Film (New York: Oxford University Press, 1974), page 97.

[5]Andrew Sarris, "The American Cinema," Film Culture, No. 28 (Spring, 1963), page 3.

[6]Patricia Jaffe, "Editing Cinéma Vérité," Film Comment, III, No. 3 (Summer, 1965), page 43.

[7]"Table-Ronde: Festival de Tours en Collaboration l'U. N. E. S. C. O.," Image et Son, No. 160 (Mars, 1963), page 6.

[8]Ibid.

[9]Flaherty, op. cit., page 21.

[10]Ibid., page 40.

[11]James Blue, "Thoughts on Cinéma Vérité," Film Comments, Vol. 2, No. 4 (Fall, 1965), page 23.

[12]Nicholas Roger Clapp, "The Naturalistic Documentary, 1896-1960" (unpublished Master's Thesis, Department of Cinema, University of Southern California, Los Angeles, August, 1962), pages 43-47.

CHAPTER IV

NEO-REALISM

The art of cinema has gone through constant changes
in its comparatively short life. Filmic trends and styles
have appeared and vanished; new movements have started,
enjoyed a period of popularity and then have disappeared.
Some have put their permanent stamp on the art of cinema,
others have faded away. Each, however, has left its influence on the ones that followed it; each new trend and style
has refined and updated the previous one to correspond to the
society it served. The over-riding tendency of cinema since
1945, however, has been to push further and further toward
cinematic realism. Great social, educational, technical and
artistic changes in the past three decades have given impetus
to this rapid development.

Following the Second World War, two different movements appeared in Europe which indirectly influenced the
emergence of cinéma vérité: neo-realism and nouvelle vague.
Neo-realism was a revolutionary cinematic movement that
originated in Italy. The films in this movement began to
deal with realistic subject matter rather than with pure dramatic fantasy. It is believed that Luchino Visconti, with his
truthful treatment of everyday Italian life in his Ossessione
(1942), laid the foundation of the Italian school of neo-realism.
In 1945 Roberto Rossellini, with Roma, Citta Aperta ("Rome,
Open City"), introduced the credo of the neo-realistic movement to the entire world, as did Vittoria De Sica in his
Sciuscia ("Shoeshine") in 1946. Other great film-makers
such as Zavattini, Fellini and Antonioni followed suit.

The movement was paralleled in other film-making
countries of Europe. According to Roger Manvell, in
France realism came with René Clément's La Bataille du
Rail ('Railway Battle,' 1945) and was further developed in
1947 in Claude Autant-Lara's Le Diable du Corps. [1] In
Poland, Wanda Jacobowski's film Auschwitz, the Last Stage

(1948) was a revealing attempt toward realism. In Germany, neo-realism started with Die Morder Sind Unter Uns ("The Murderers Are Among Us," 1946) by Wolfgang Staudte; in Switzerland with The Search (1948) by Fred Zinneman. In Britain realism appeared strongly in war films, and in 1956 in a movement called "Free Cinema." Realism also appeared in American crime and gangster films, not to mention those handling war subjects.

Cinema, one of the most influential and popular arts, has always helped to create as well as to reflect the cultural attitude it serves. But it can only induce changes which the society itself is ready to adopt. In the treatment of war subjects, popular in the mid-forties, audiences who had ex-perienced the war at first hand demanded a more realistic treatment of stories about the war, in style closer to the documentary approach than to that of the polished feature film. The new film-makers, therefore, diverted from the conventional style to a cinematic presentation that showed audiences as true a portrait of themselves and their sur-roundings as possible, enabling them, somewhat in line with Flaherty's concept, to identify with the characters on the screen.

When one considers theatrical films produced prior to World War II, Italian neo-realism emerges as a great revo-lution towards truthfulness in cinema. Reviewing the feature films made during the 1930s and early 1940s on both sides of the Atlantic, Roger Manvell says,

> ... Films were delivered in well-shaped paragraphs or sequences, while the actors only too often ca-pered through their dialogue like well-drilled, highly professional dummies. [2]

The non-realist movement in essence freed cinema from old conventional methods of film-making, breathed new life into it, expanded and humanized it and thus brought it closer to life itself. For example, in "Rome, Open City" (a film about the Nazi occupation of Rome during World War II), Roberto Rossellini used in supporting roles ordinary peo-ple who could bring their actual experience under the Nazi rule of Rome onto the screen. He photographed most of his exterior shots (during the occupation) from a high vantage point, showing German soldiers in the streets below.

Vittoria De Sica's The Bicycle Thief is a story of a

working man whose livelihood depends on his bicycle. At the
moment when a job he has been seeking for some time mate-
rializes, he finds a thief has made off with his treasured bicycle. The film depicts the desperate search by the poor
man and his son for the vehicle. It is a story of the struggle for existence in a world that seems totally indifferent to
the dire plight of any one lone man. In this poignant film,
De Sica used non-professional actors; the son is played by a
newsboy, and the father by an ordinary working man. The
setting is actually a poor section of Rome; the story line is
taken from real life in the Italy of the time.

In pursuit of cinematic realism, the Italian neo-realist
movement borrowed some of the concepts manifested by Dziga
Vertov and separated itself from the conventional cinema's
approach of make-believe. Roger Manvell, writing about
Visconti's film <u>Ossessione</u>, says it portrayed

> ... the deep attachment to the vitality of the work-
> ing-class life ... and the determination to show how
> poverty, overcrowding and sordid living-conditions
> affect the humanity of men, women and children
> alike. [3]

These cinematic changes were not restricted to subject
matter and characterization; they also affected techniques in
film production. The camera lost its position as merely a
video recorder and became an instrument of direct creation
which could explore the world in a more realistic fashion.
Photography became expressive rather than merely mechani-
cally functional. Studio sets were abandoned as far as possible in favor of natural locations. Hand-held cameras, permitting ease of movement, were used increasingly; and, like
Vertov, some film-makers concealed their cameras to obtain
truthful and realistic shots.

As the trend in film-making changed from a preoccupation with war subjects to those dealing with peace, the
emphasis on realism, well established in Europe and the
United States by 1950, moved with it.

The Italians, who were the first to concern themselves
with topics other than those dealing with war, turned to the
pursuit of subjects that had to do with the problems of ordinary people in their daily life.

The horrors attendant upon chronic unemployment were

reflected in The Bicycle Thief of De Sica and Visconti's La Terre Treme ("The Earth Trembles"), 1958. The latter dramatically portrayed the unsuccessful efforts of a Sicilian family to own their own fishing boat. This treatment of subject matter was further reinforced in 1952 when De Sica presented Umberto D, a film dealing with the frustration and humiliation of a retired man used to better things in life and now attempting to exist on a pitifully inadequate pension.

This new trend in cinema was, therefore, not simply something created on paper to reflect the scriptwriter's point of view; rather, it was based on real life experience, photographed and presented as true to life as possible. As one writer aptly put it, it was hand-made as against factory-made.

Cesare Zavattini says of neo-realism "there must be no gap between life and what is on the screen," and adds, "I am bored to death with heroes more or less imaginary. I want to meet the real protagonist of everyday life. I want to see how he is made, if he has a moustache or not, if he is tall or short. I want to see his eyes, and I want to speak to him." Summing up his point somewhat, he says, "Neo-realism has perceived that the most irreplaceable experience comes from things happening under our own eyes from natural necessity. "[4]

And thus, with the emergence of neo-realism in Italy, films became the personal expressions of their directors rather than episodes first viewed and distilled by a writer's perhaps narrow experience and background. Films became the cinema d'auteurs, rather than products of the traditional studio.

The conventional film, which continued to be the staying power of cinema as an entertainment medium with its dramatic fantasy approach, was not wiped out by the emergence of this style, but it was greatly influenced by the innovations of the new movement.

It should be noted that the influence of neo-realism on cinéma vérité is rather remote and indirect; there is an analogy rather than a kinship between the two. Although both are primarily interested in presenting reality, cinéma vérité advocates no reconstruction of reality, whereas the aim of neo-realism is to provide a completely faithful artistic and dramatic reconstruction of reality. Neo-realism makes no effort to seize the event as it actually happens, while the whole philosophy of cinéma vérité revolves around this aspect. Neo-realism is not concerned with capturing spontaneous action; to the cinéma vérité film-maker, if the material is not spontaneous, it cannot be true. The aim of the cinéma vérité film-maker is simply to record what is there as he sees it. And since such films are less formal and more episodic, they naturally demand more participation on the part of the audience. In this sense, cinéma vérité is closer to neo-realism than to the classical documentary, and this is why the Italians see it as only one of the particular forms of neo-realism and reject the need for a distinct term. As was mentioned in Chapter I, the Italians felt that if it were necessary to use a label for this style, they would call it "film inquiry."

It might be said, however--although it is an oversimplification--that neo-realism tries to achieve a "dramatized reality" of social and everday life, while cinéma vérité seeks pure reality, untampered with. Neo-realism's frank approach to human problems stimulated a public taste for authenticity and laid the groundwork for the emerging cinéma vérité philosophy of "capturing reality."

NOTES

[1]Roger Manvell, New Cinema in Europe (New York: E. P. Dutton and Co., Inc., 1966), pages 16-17.

[2]Ibid., page 15.

[3]Ibid., page 18.

[4]Cesare Zavattini, "Some Ideas on the Cinema," Sight and Sound, Vol. 23, No. 1 (July-September, 1953), page 68.

CHAPTER V

NOUVELLE VAGUE

The neo-realist movement in Italy forced film-making
toward a more realistic treatment of the subject matter, and
thus closer to the realities of everyday life.   Yet this style
did not deeply influence French cinema.   The French did,
however, make a number of "realist" films after the war
which went beyond "mere superficial 'likeness' in portrayal
of people and places" and moved toward a "more imaginative
understanding of what realism can mean when it is taken beyond" this concept. [1]   During the decade after World War II,
a number of French film-makers, influenced by the emergence of realism in cinema, took the concept further and
created a new style known as nouvelle vague (the "new wave").

Nouvelle vague was born in the mid-fifties with a number of young cinema enthusiasts who were either film critics
(the Cahiers du Cinéma group) or came from documentary
and short film productions.   "In fact, the nucleus essentially
consisted of the critical team of Cahiers du Cinéma, who in
their writings had defined and energetically sustained a
'politique des auteurs. '"[2]

Claude Chabrol, Jean-Luc Godard, and François Truffaut were among the nouvelle vague directors who came from
the group of critics writing for Cahiers du Cinéma, while
Agnes Varda, Jean Rouch, Mario Ruspoli and Chris Marker
established themselves through the production of documentaries and short films.   Most of these new directors had not
served the conventional apprenticeship in film-making; in fact,
some had never made a film.   The Cahiers group, for example, had learned the techniques of film production simply
by reviewing films.   Others with some experience in film-
making took their simplified and personalized approaches
(learned from short films and documentaries) to feature
films, and thereby moved away from the conventional and
technical complexities of the past.   Due to their lack of tech-

nical know-how, the attitude of these young directors toward film-making was to keep it as simple as possible. They sought to separate themselves from the over-professionalism and over-technicality which often handicap the inspiration of the film-maker. Most of these new directors, in particular the Cahiers du Cinéma group, being mainly writers, started using the camera (with all its technical complexities) as an author uses his typewriter.

The philosophy of Italian neo-realism was to move toward a realistic treatment of the film content while on the whole remaining faithful to the principal grammar of conventional cinema. The nouvelle vague movement, however, rebelled against both film content and the conventional techniques utilized in traditional cinema. Its practitioners introduced procedures into film-making which, up to that time, were uncommon in the theatrical cinema: free photography, improvisation in acting, jump-cuts in editing, working without a shooting script, etc.

When these rebellious young directors presented some of their films at the Cannes Film Festival in 1959, their approach to film-making was dubbed la nouvelle vague by their journalistic colleagues, and thus a new style in cinema was christened. According to Jonas Mekas,

> ... skyrocketing into public attention during the last Cannes film festival, this 'wave'--including François Truffaut, Claude Chabrol, Alain Resnais, Marcel Camus, Jean Rouch, Louis Malle, among others-- suddenly became public property. And whereas it usually was three to four years before an 'art' film got to the United States, it took no longer than two months for the films of the New Wave to reach the American shore. [3]

Mekas dated the birth of the movement with the appearance of Françoise Sagan, Roger Vadim and Brigitte Bardot. "Sagan and Vadim were the first ones to sum up the mores and dreams of their contemporaries, and by pushing them into an irrational emotional extreme--the same way Elvis Presley pushed the lust for materiality ... by purchasing four cars--made their contemporaries see the absurdity and decadence of those mores and those dreams. "[4]

Where and by whom or through what means the movement started and developed is not the issue. The important consideration is that a number of dedicated, though inexperienced, film-makers in France broke away from the old traditions and principles in cinema and created a "new wave," one that influenced the state of the art of film-making both in Europe and the United States.

In their quest for individuality, these film-makers accorded no importance to the studio, the scriptwriter or the scenario; they maintained that it was the director who became the sole creative source in the making of a film and who should have complete control over it. It was "cinema in which the conscious plan is no longer visible, cinema as a fluid personal expression, a fluidity punctuated only by the temperament of the film-maker himself. "[5]

These new directors were able to prove that it was possible to produce commercially successful films without the big studios, without name stars, with small crews, and by shooting on location with minimum professional technical support--a daring approach. Their style in film-making was cinematically simplistic.

Truffaut, when making Les Quatre Cents Coup, described his method thus:

> I work practically without a shooting-script;
> all I prepare is the dialogue. And when I have
> scenes too delicate to be shot in the usual way--
> like Antoine's scene with the psychologist--I clear
> everybody out and lock myself in alone with the
> actors and the cameraman. You can't put the best
> moments of a film down in the script. [6]

Godard made his famous film Breathless (1959) from a three-page script outline by Truffaut, with no scenario in the old-fashioned sense. The film deals with a situation involving a petty swaggering gangster, Michel, and a young American girl, Patricia, who hawks Herald-Tribunes on the streets of Paris. The disarmingly charming Michel steals a car and kills a police-patrol. Patricia, with whom he is having a love affair, has tired of him, and so betrays him to the authorities to get rid of him. Showing little emotion, Michel dies under police fire.

The actors improvised their dialogue under Godard's supervision during the filming and it is so sparse that one reviewer commented that it almost gives one the feeling of eavesdropping. Edoardo Bruno said of this director, "Godard acts on his characters without intermediary, but he rigorously controls their reactions and the results in order to achieve an expressive end. "[7]

During the editing of Breathless, Godard introduced his celebrated jump-cuts to force the pace of the action of the film, which moves at a high pitch of tension.

Charlotte and Her Jules, made in 1958 with Jean-Paul Belmondo, is a prime example of Godard's approach, and of the nouvelle vague philosophy, when one considers it was shot during one afternoon in his apartment at a cost of only $1,000.

Another of Godard's films done in this style is Une Femme Est une Femme ("A Woman Is a Woman")--considered by some to be his best--in which he allows total improvisation by his actors. This amusing film is the story of a girl who has written letters to two of her lovers, breaking a rendezvous with one and arranging to see the other. Thinking she has made a terrible mistake by misaddressing them so that each will get the wrong note, she attempts to extricate herself from her web. However, the notes were addressed correctly and, appearing ridiculous to her lovers, she loses both.

Marcorelles says about Godard's use of improvisation that he "seeks to flush out reality, to catch on the wing expressions and attitudes which, better than any dialogue, can reveal a person's psychology and the dramatic significance of a situation. "[8]

In photography also, the nouvelle vague directors were opposed to the smooth, polished film of the past; their method favored realistic visual representation rather than pretty, well-lighted, well-composed shots. And as was mentioned, Godard's jump-cut technique in editing is a product of the nouvelle vague school.

In short, the nouvelle vague method aimed at "... the break-up of the old-fashioned, artificial 'well-made' film about 'well-made' characters, and the emergence of a style of direction operating in free association with real-life characters, many of whom seemed to have been met casually in the street. "[9]

The "new wave" approach to film-making influenced a number of film-makers both in Europe and the United States to experiment further with the techniques of the new style. Their efforts resulted in the emergence of yet another new movement in cinema which in France, upon the release of Rouch's Chronique d'un Eté, was christened "cinéma vérité." In the United States, this movement, which grew out of the traditions of nouvelle vague, was called "direct cinema."

Manvell, discussing nouvelle vague, comments:

> The vocabulary and grammar of the conventional film were replaced by something new--either inspired or uninspired improvisation in which film-makers such as Jean Rouch experimented in Chronique d'un Eté (1961).... In addition, the films associated particularly with Chris Marker (Cuba Si, 1961; Le Joli Mai, 1963) introduced cine-verite, a technique of film-making dependent on using the recently developed lightweight equipment.... [10]

Nouvelle vague established a completely new concept of film structure which, with the development of portable, synchronous sound equipment, led to the emergence of cinéma vérité in France. But it should be noted that although cinéma vérité was an offshoot of nouvelle vague and developed along the lines of this school, its aim, contrary to that of nouvelle vague, is to present the "truth."

The influence of nouvelle vague on cinéma vérité, therefore, should be considered only operational. This new grammar, however, inspired film-makers such as Jean Rouch, Jacques Rozier and Chris Marker, most of whom were trained in the nouvelle vague movement, to experiment with the new freedom in film-making, and with the help of newly developed portable equipment, to produce films such as Chronique d'un Eté, Adieu Philippine, [11] and Le Joli Mai, which, although listed as nouvelle vauge films, have also become classical examples of the cinéma vérité school.

NOTES

[1]Roger Manvell, New Cinema in Europe (New York: E. P. Dutton and Co., Inc., 1966), page 7.

[2]Jacques Siclier, "New Wave and French Cinema," Sight and Sound, XXX, No. 3 (Summer, 1961), page 116.

[3]Jonas Mekas, "Cinema of the New Generation," (Part One: "Free Cinema and the Nouvelle Vague") Film Culture, No. 21 (Summer, 1960), page 1.

[4]Ibid., page 5.

[5]Ibid. page 4.

[6]Manvell, op. cit., page 69.

[7]Edoardo Bruno, "Prospects of Direct Cinema in Relation to Film Language," Filmcritica, Vol. XVII, No. 163 (January, 1966), page 4.

[8]Louis Marcorelles, "Jean-Luc Godard's Half Truths," Film Quarterly, Vol. XVII, No. 3 (Spring, 1964), page 7.

[9]Manvell, op. cit., pages 78-79.

[10]Ibid.

[11]Considered "the Nouvelle Vague's finest achievement"--Ian Cameron and Mark Shivas, "Interviews," Movie, No. 8 (April, 1963), page 23. (Interview with Jacques Rozier.)

CHAPTER VI

THE FREE CINEMA

In England, meanwhile, another movement known as Free Cinema took root, and was part of the whole European trend toward realism and against the artificiality of the conventional cinema. Although a relatively small and short-lived movement, it was another factor that served to support the emergence of cinéma vérité in the 1960s.

Like nouvelle vague, which received some of its impetus from writers in Cahiers du Cinéma, Free Cinema received its main inspiration from a magazine called Sequence, which began as an Oxford University publication in 1949 and terminated in 1952 after the production of 14 issues.

The editors, Lindsay Anderson and Gavin Lambert (and later Karel Reisz and Penelope Houston), severely criticized British cinema for persistently ignoring regional culture and presenting only the image of a pre-1914 bourgeoisie. Quoting from Sequence:

> For the failure of Britain to achieve, in fifty years of picture making any considerable tradition of cinema ... many and varied reasons have been suggested. One seldom stressed but surely among the most relevant, is the influence of Class. The British commercial cinema has been a bourgeois rather than a revolutionary growth; and it is not a middle-class trait to examine oneself with the strictest objectivity, or to be able to represent higher or lower levels of society with sympathy and respect.

The writer continues to say,

> ... it has been the function of the working-classes to provide 'comic relief' to the sufferings of their social superiors, or to nip in here and there with

Dramatic Cameos; at any rate to support self-
consciously rather than spontaneously to pre-figure. [1]

The label "Free Cinema" was introduced when the National Film Theater of London presented a program of short
films under that title in February of 1956.   Along with a
short story film Together, by an Italian, Lorenz Mazzetti,
the program included films produced by two men who had at-
tacked British cinema from the pages of their magazine
Sequence: O Dreamland by Lindsay Anderson and Momma
Don't Allow by Karel Reisz and Tony Richardson.

Program notes for this first presentation of Free Cinema offer an explanation for the term as well as motives behind the movement:

> The film makers of 'Free Cinema' prefer to
> call their work 'free' rather than 'experimental.'
> It is neither introverted nor esoteric.   Nor is the
> concern primarily with technique.   These films are
> free in the sense that their statements are entirely
> personal.   Though their moods and subjects differ,
> the concern of each of them is with some aspect
> of life as it is lived in this country today....
>
> Implicit in our attitude is a belief in freedom,
> in the importance of people and in the significance
> of the everyday. [2]

For the first time, these films showed images of London as it was--with its streets, dance halls and entertainment places at night, its playgrounds and warehouses.   Actors in these films were real people, going about their day-
to-day business--no glamorized actors, no stars, and none
of the pomp and show of the conventional cinema.   One could
see a certain freshness in these films because they depicted
the real environment of the people of London.

O Dreamland takes its title from the amusement park
bearing the name "Dreamland," the setting for the picture.
The film-makers attempted to portray the superficiality of
the desperate gropings for pleasure through the cheap popular
entertainment found at such a place.   The background music
is raucous and offensive.

Momma Don't Allow reveals life on an ordinary evening at a jazz club.   A slight thread of plot involves three

characters (a cleaning girl, a hairdresser and a butcher) who meet their partners and join some "Teddy Boys" for an evening of somewhat frenzied dancing.

Together is somewhat different, for it followed a scenario and shooting script of 80 pages approved by the British Film Institute. It portrays the isolation and mental suffering of two deaf-mutes (employed as dock-workers) who are subjected to the impatience and indifference of adults and the taunts of cruel, thoughtless children on the street. The end of the film, as one of the men who has been accidentally pushed off a bridge drowns, is shocking; the surviving deaf-mute realizes he must now "go it alone."

Nice Time, by Alain Tanner and Claude Goretta, another film in the Free Cinema movement, depicts the activities of a group of people--dancers, musicians, slummers, ordinary people--"out on the town" in search of a good time on Saturday night in Piccadilly Circus.

Perhaps the best-known of the Free Cinema films that initiated the movement in England is Every Day Except Christmas, by Lindsay Anderson, Leon Clore and Karel Reisz (1957), a film about the life of the night workers at London's early morning market in Covent Garden--a life which for centuries has continued night after night, except Christmas. The film takes the viewer somewhere far out in the English countryside where men are loading their lorries with flowers and food, driving out into the night toward London at about the time the BBC announcer is signing off. The film, "can remind the jaded movie-goer of the incredible riches of daily life."[3]

The program introducing this film declared:

> This program is not put before you as an achievement but as an aim. We ask you to view it not as critics, nor as a diversion, but in direct relation to a British cinema still obstinately class-bound, still rejecting the stimulus of contemporary life, as well as the responsibility to criticize; still reflecting a metropolitan, Southern English culture which excludes the rich diversity of tradition and personality which is the whole of Britain.[4]

In describing this film Rudolph Arnheim speaks of a world of boxes and crates irrationally stacked, of fatiguing endlessness, noises, milling crowds, rapid turnover of in-

numerable objects and passersby--all adding up to an even
texture of unceasing disorder "cut from the loom of time
more or less at random."[5]

Anderson and his two associates show the well-dressed
man in the market who gives orders with authority and with
little thought about price, as well as the timid, itinerant
merchant who hesitates before making choices because he has
little money. The poor people pick up discarded, damaged
fruits and vegetables, and finally the lorries are loaded with
empty crates and depart to the areas from which they came.

Following these initial films, Karel Reisz was able to
persuade the Ford Motor Company to subsidize other films
to be produced in the spirit and technique of Free Cinema.
Mr. Reisz himself directed We Are the Lambeth Boys (1958),
a revealing study of the life of teenagers in a South London
youth club.

Rudolph Arnheim summed it up rather well: Free
Cinema films "are small injections of reality. It is the life
of the manual worker ... the unobtrusive pedestrian, the
anonymous population, life on the unredeemed battlefield of
the ruins of the slums of London."[6]

As is often the case when new ideas emerge, some
critics disagreed with the approach of the Free Cinema film-
makers.

Paul Rotha and Richard Griffith, in their book, The
Film Till Now, A Survey of World Cinema, write:

> Although the pictures from this group [Free
> Cinema film-makers] have been over-praised--
> largely because so much orthodox British documen-
> tary has become pedestrian--Lindsay Anderson's
> 'Every Day Except Christmas' (1957) had a lively
> style and a candid-camera technique which made it
> worthwhile and Karel Reisz's 'We Are the Lambeth
> Boys' (1958) had a vitality and an authenticity so
> badly lacking in the great majority of British fea-
> ture productions.[7]

Denis Horne was one who felt that these film-makers
took themselves too seriously. Expressing his opinion in a
magazine article entitled "The Free Cinema Hoax," he called
the whole movement "still-born."[8]

In another article, Lewis Jacobs was a bit kinder in his criticism of Together (Horne and Mazzetti):

> In the film makers' ruthless attempt to avoid any narrative or dramatic structure, which might have emotionalized the incidents, the scenes became drawn out and monotonous, the tempo tedious; the sequences lacked climax, and often ended abruptly. [9]

Whether or not the critics were justified in their criticism, the Free Cinema film-makers did turn the camera eye on everyday life in their society, somewhat in line with Vertov's theories. And, for the first time in the British cinema, film-makers showed their audiences, "This is the world in which we live." Like Vertov, they sometimes used candid camera techniques, but later edited their films, adding sound at will to put across ideas not necessarily present in the original situations.

The next step in British cinema in its return to reality was the adaptation of novels and stage plays in the spirit of Free Cinema. Jack Clayton was among the first with his adaptation of John Braine's novel, Room at the Top (1959) and Tony Richardson's adaptation of the stage play, Look Back in Anger.

Two years later Karel Reisz presented an adaptation of Alan Sillitoe's novel, Saturday Night and Sunday Morning, and in 1963 Lindsay Anderson directed a film, This Sporting Life, based on David Storey's novel. Reporting this activity in British films, David Robinson writes:

> In this way, borrowing the titles and subjects of successful new novels and the new drama, the British cinema treated--for the first time it seemed --subjects of authentic regional and working class life. These first films were a success, and eventually there was a rush to imitate them. For a year or so practically every director took his turn at what were dubbed 'kitchen sink' films, but for all the cheapening of the new spirit into a commercial genre, the revolution had been accomplished. [10]

With the development of Free Cinema style, things that before seemed to be of no concern to film-makers and of little interest to film viewers assumed importance for the pioneers of this movement in England. By treating such ordinary subjects, they encouraged film-makers both in Europe and the United States to experiment more freely with this medium, and influenced them to break away further from the old traditions (as had their predecessors in neo-realism and nouvelle vague), going to life itself for their material.

The Free Cinema movement in England thus further paved the way for the emergence of cinéma vérité.

NOTES

[1] David Robinson, The History of World Cinema (New York: Stein and Day, 1973), pages 291-292.

[2] Ibid., page 294.

[3] Rudolph Arnheim, "Free Cinema II," Film Culture, IV, No. 2 (17), (February, 1958), page 11.

[4] Robinson, op. cit., pages 294-295.

[5] Arnheim, loc. cit.

[6] Arnheim, loc. cit.

[7] Paul Rotha and Richard Griffith, The Film Till Now, A Survey of World Cinema (London: Spring Books, 1967), page 735.

[8] Denis Horne, "The Free Cinema Hoax," Film Journal, No. 17 (April, 1961), page 109.

[9] Lewis Jacobs, "Free Cinema 1," Film Culture, IV, No. 2 (17), (February, 1958), page 10.

[10] Robinson, op. cit., page 296.

CHAPTER VII

TELEVISION

From the time television was commercially established
in the 1940s until 1952, most television presentations consisted of live programs--programs which had very little in
common and often displayed no program continuity. As Ray
Sipherd says, "... it attempted to be all things to all people.
A Toscanini concert was followed by the Roller Derby, and
a performance of 'Macbeth' with wrestling. "[1]

Technology not having advanced sufficiently in the television industry, simultaneous transmission of events presented
many difficult or unsolvable problems.   Concurrent and universal televising of a man's walk on the moon or showing the
American presidential election returns in those early years
would have made the engineer's hair turn gray.

In 1952, Carl Kramer, working for M.C.A., Inc.,
came up with the idea of putting television programs on films.
The first one cost $4,000 and was sold to a watch company. [2]
Following this effort the filmed program became the most
desirable form of telecasting. It was easy to repeat the program at any time, play it on other stations, and above all
it provided better control of what went on the air.

From the very start, however, television adopted
16mm film for most of its location coverage; it was more
economical than 35mm film and easier to handle. As a result, 16mm film and equipment advanced from amateur to
professional status almost overnight.   Nevertheless, when
television adopted the 16mm format, it also borrowed cinema's production techniques, together with its cumbersome
equipment and huge staff.   The 16mm equipment designed for
professional film-making, although smaller and more economical than 35mm, still had the major disadvantages of its elder
brother; it was heavy, difficult to move around and noisy
without a blimp. As Mario Ruspoli nicely put it, the blimp

"turned the camera into a monstrous piece of artillery which needed several attendants whenever it had to be moved. Reloading when the film was used up meant opening the blimp, a time-consuming operation which destroyed the continuity of the shot at the expense, of course, of its homogeneity."[3]

Furthermore, television had to operate at a much faster pace than cinema in order to meet its strict deadlines. Cumbersome equipment and time-consuming procedures and techniques in cinema, slowing down the process of film-making, had to be changed. Lightweight, easy-to-handle equipment and rapid and direct approaches to film production had to be sought.

"Yet, as television grew, it discovered that its greatest talents--those in which no other medium could challenge it--were the immediacy and intimacy with which it could record contemporary events,"[4] and its most important tasks, to entertain and to inform. Because of its large daily program requirements, and because television became a more and more important medium of information, it had to go directly to life itself for its cogent material. Popular subjects such as sports, politics and news had to be covered on the spot for presentation at an early showing for viewers.

As a first step toward the accomplishment of this task, television developed mobile teams for location coverage of events, although still using the same bulky equipment and a large staff, often carried in two or three vehicles. Photographing events spontaneously on location was much more difficult than shooting in the studio, where everything was under the control of the film-makers.

One of the more serious problems was the synchronous recording of sound with picture while maintaining complete mobility. The immediacy of events to be covered and the deadlines to be met in television made the principle of post-synchronization, as known in cinema, out of the question. Efforts were made, therefore, to reduce the technical complexity of film-making on location and, in particular, the synchronous recording of sound with picture as far as possible. Television, in this regard, deserves the credit for having been the first to tackle the problem of mobile synchronous cinematography and of acquiring portable, noiseless 16mm equipment.[5]

Responding to this demand, manufacturers started to

develop 16mm lightweight cameras and portable tape recorders. By 1960 such equipment was sufficiently advanced to
enable a team of two, a cameraman and a sound-man, to go
into any situation and photograph any event in sychronization.
So it was that the television requirement for portable cameras
and tape recorders expedited the development of lightweight
equipment for synchronous filming--the prerequisite for the
emergence of the cinéma vérité movement. Television, from
its inception, also played an important part in the evolution
of cinematic techniques, and influenced the art and technique
of film-making.

    Jean Renoir, in an interview with André Bazin, speak-
ing of a film version of Stevenson's Dr. Jekyll and Mr. Hyde
which he was making for television, said:

> I would like to make this film--and this is
> where television gives me something valuable--in
> the spirit of live television. I'd like to make the
> film as though it were a live broadcast, shooting
> each scene only once, with the actors imagining
> that the public are directly receiving their words
> and gestures. Both the actors and the technicians
> should know that there will be no retakes; that,
> whether they succeed or not, they can't begin
> again. [6]

    Renoir then added, "I'd like to break with cinema tech-
nique, and very patiently build a large wall with little
stones." In chapters to follow, contributions made by American and French film-makers in developing new cinematic
techniques, particularly in the area of documentaries for television, will be discussed briefly.

    With the development of the new portable equipment
for television, film-makers began to break away from certain
established cinematic techniques and started experimenting
with new styles. For example, the ABC-TV News documentary series Close-Up! was initiated in September, 1960 with
Cast the First Stone, which dealt with racial prejudice in
the North. It wielded a powerful influence and did much to
pave the way for subsequent efforts of similar import.

    In the summer of 1962, the Maysles brothers and
Hillary Harris made a film for CBS covering a "meeting of
minds" between Archibald MacLeish and Mark Van Doren.
The filming, done over a week-end, followed vérité tech-

niques. However, some critics believe that not enough respect was given to the intellectual content of the dialogue.
The camera roved restlessly over objects in the area, such
as the table and coffee pot, while one of the men propounded
his opinion on a very serious subject. Attention was dis-
tracted from the very core of the intellectual give-and-take.

NBC's Special Projects established a series (for Purex)
in 1961-1962 entitled The World of _____ . Chief
responsibility for the series was given to Eugene S. Jones,
who gathered an able crew about him to assist in the endeav-
or. Well-known personalities featured in the series were
Jacqueline Kennedy, Jimmy Doolittle, Benny Goodman, Sophia
Loren, Maurice Chevalier, Darryl F. Zanuck and Billy Graham.

> Particularly startling was a devastating scene
> in a Manchester pub in the Billy Graham story.
> This stark vérité record of the tragedy of small
> lives in a fierce world showed how powerfully the
> unobtrusive camera can operate in that situation
> where noise, smoke and liquor have dulled human
> sensibilities to that point at which, if the subject
> is aware of the camera at all, he regards it as a
> roistering companion. In the white-masked face of
> the pub songstress there was little human charac-
> teristic whatever. No other depiction of despair
> could have set the contrast for Billy Graham's ex-
> hortation to Manchesterians [sic] nearly so well. [7]

Cinéma vérité, then, was a direct beneficiary of filming techniques which had to be innovated in television in order to achieve reality and immediacy of news coverage,
sports events, interviews, documentaries, etc. Roy Armes,
in his book French Cinema Since 1946, states, "In essence,
Cinéma-Vérité is an attempt to bring to the cinema the
freer reporting methods of television...."[8]

Aesthetically, however, television is responsible for
introducing a "direct style which reveals the charm of the
present,"[9] thereby helping educate public tastes to appreciate
this approach. Thus, "in this sense, it has been a 'pace-
setter' in the trend towards reality."[10] Both television and
cinéma vérité, in "trapping a moment of reality" in an interview, for example, have the same characteristics of present-
tense, the essence of the image being something direct.
Each holds in common with the other a preoccupation with

objectivity, the inclination to remove itself from what we are seeing. But cinéma vérité tries to go a step further than its antecedents. As one writer put it, "it dreams of a cinema without a cinema"--a reality purged of all intervention by the film-maker.

But what of the cinéma vérité film exposure to the public? Although in France attempts have been made to blow up 16mm vérité films for exhibition in the theatrical cinema, few of them gain by being shown on the big screen, where their technical defects only loom larger. The small screen of television seems to be a logical outlet through which cinéma vérité films can commercially survive. It is for this reason, perhaps, that Norman Swallow in his Factual Television calls cinéma vérité tele-vérité.

Flipping through the pages of the history of world cinema, one finds that Vertov introduced the philosophy of portraying real life rather than dramatic fantasy on the screen. Then Flaherty, his contemporary, experimented with this philosophy, manipulating his film, primarily in shooting, to leave the fullest scientific record of a culture, using actual people in their natural location. Neo-realism in Italy established a frank approach to human problems, stimulating a public taste for authenticity in theatrical films. Nouvelle vague, in France, rebelled against the conventional rules and grammar of theatrical cinema and introduced previously unheard of practices such as working without a shooting script, improvisation in acting, free photography, and jump-cuts in editing. With this approach, film-makers maintained that the director was the sole creative force in making a film. Free cinema film-makers combined many of these concepts in their approach, focusing their attention on the importance of common people and the significance of everyday life, but scorning the traditional practice of presenting only the image of Britain's upper class, particularly the pre-1914 bourgeoisie. Television, because of its unique requirements, forced the industry to produce simpler equipment and more advanced technology in cinema, enabling film-makers to photograph and record in synchronization with much freedom, making it possible to capture life as it was lived.

The philosophy, styles, techniques and varied approaches of Vertov, Flaherty, neo-realism, nouvelle vague, free cinema and finally television, all contributed to bringing about the movement in cinema which was, in the early sixties, named cinéma vérité.

NOTES

[1]Ray Sipherd, "The Long Courtship: Films of Social Inquiry for Television," Film Comment, Vol. 2, No. 1 (Winter, 1964), p. 18.

[2]Personal interview with Herb Stern, Head of Legal Department, M. C. A., Inc., March, 1967.

[3]Mario Ruspoli, "Toward a New Film Technique in the Developing Countries: The Light-Weight Synchronized Cinematographic Unit," U. N. E. S. C. O. Report, October, 1963 (translated and mimeographed), pages 5-6.

[4]Sipherd, loc. cit.

[5]Ruspoli, loc. cit.

[6]André Bazin, "Jean Renoir and Roberto Rossellini interviewed by André Bazin," (Cinema and Television), Sight and Sound, Vol. 28, No. 1 (Winter, 1958/1959), page 26.

[7]A. William Bleum, Documentary in American Television (New York: Hastings House, Communication Arts Books, 1965), page 186.

[8]Roy Armes, French Cinema since 1946, Vol. II: The Personal Style (Amsterdam: Drukkerijen vh., Ellerman Harms NV, 1966), pages 124-125.

[9]Jean-Claude Bringuier, "Libres Propos sur le Cinéma-Vérité," Cahiers du Cinéma, Vol. XXV, No. 145 (Juillet, 1963), page 14.

[10]Ibid.

PART III:

THE TWO SCHOOLS OF CINEMA VERITE

CHAPTER VIII

JEAN ROUCH: THE FRENCH SCHOOL

Looking at the cinéma vérité movement in the fifties
and sixties, one can see two major schools developing around
this style: a French school and an American school. The
approach of Jean Rouch, with whom the name cinéma vérité
is directly associated, may well represent the French school
of this movement. To understand this school it is essential
to know Jean Rouch and his style of film-making.

Rouch stepped into cinema almost in the same way as
Flaherty, one of his three mentors.[1] Born in Paris (May
31, 1917), he went into civil engineering and specialized in
the building of bridges and roads. Later he became an ethnographer and worked at the Musée de l'Homme in Paris.
Being influenced by his anthropology teacher at the Sorbonne,
who believed that cinema was the best tool with which to
study ethnography, Rouch used a camera to record his ethnographical work in Africa, and gradually became more and
more interested in film-making.

In 1946, on his first expedition to the Niger River,
he took a 16mm Bell and Howell camera with which he photographed hippopotamus-hunting (Chasse à l'Hippopotame, 1948);
the result later proved to be more than a documentary film,
for it also had a story line. When he returned to Paris, a
producer became interested in his film and decided to edit
it for him. It was during this collaboration that Rouch became fascinated with the medium of cinema.

While on the expedition to photograph the hippopotamus-
hunting, he had abandoned the tripod in order to allow himself facility of movement; the resulting footage was unstable
and often difficult to watch but it was extremely interesting.
In his own words,

> When I came back there were a lot of people
> who said that the film was not good because it was
> not as steady as it could be if I had used a tripod.
> I used a tripod at first, but I discovered it was
> impossible to use one if you want to have a very
> versatile camera. I tried to be as steady as possi-
> ble, but never again used a tripod in the films I
> did. [2]

The camera's freedom to move right into the action
and follow the event created a new excitement for the viewer.
As a result of this mobility, Rouch's film became unique
among anthropological films.

Some have claimed that Jean Rouch was the first to
abandon the tripod when he photographed Chasse à l'Hippopotame, but the claim is without foundation. The technique was
utilized long before by D. W. Griffith, Billy Bitzer, other
American cameramen, and most notably in Germany after
World War I. Herbert Luft, in a magazine article about
Karl Freund,[*] the notable German cameraman, says:

> ... It was the German films of that period which
> first fully demonstrated the true role of movement
> in a motion picture. The Germans did this, it is
> said, by getting the camera off the tripod and mov-
> ing it about while it was exposing film....

> ... The two films most often cited as landmarks
> of camera-movement are The Last Laugh and Va-

---

[*]Karl Freund was born in 1890 in Bohemia, from whence he
emigrated to Germany. He has said that his vital interest
in the cinema dates back to an eventful moment in childhood
when he saw a movie in which a locomotive appeared to be
heading off the screen straight into the lap of the audience.
He is credited by some for the debut of the German documentary through his production of Berlin, die Symphonie einer
Grosstadt ("Berlin, Symphony of a Big City"), made in 1927.
He did the film in "candid" style, with his hand-held camera
hidden from view as he stood on the sidewalks of Berlin or
rode on the buses through the streets. Portions of the documentary were made with his camera secured in a truck with
slots for the lens. With this approach, startlingly new at
the time, he was able to get what he considered to be a true
picture of the average inhabitant of the city.

riety. They were both photographed by Karl Freund
[in 1924].... [3]

Freund attached a small camera to his belt and swayed his
body while photographing in order to show what an intoxicated
man who has lost his equilibrium will see. In Variety he
used a swing to hold his camera, simulating a trapeze artist's
view of theater and audience. Rouch, however, abandoned
the tripod not to achieve a certain artistic effect but to free
himself to move in with the action when and as he wanted.

Later in his expeditions Rouch was one of the first to
use a portable tape recorder. In his own words,

> ... I made a film at that time recording the sound
> at the same time. That was in '51-52. Of course
> it was not exactly synchronized, but maybe the
> films were the first ones where the music and the
> sound were really authentic African music and
> sounds. This was Cimetière dans La Falaise: it
> was also part of Les Fils de l'Eau which was made
> with a lot of material done during two or three ex-
> peditions in Africa. [4]

Rouch made a number of such films in Africa, recording the sights and sounds of the native customs and religious
rites, using a free and direct approach. An important factor
in Rouch's success in capturing the authenticity of these
events was the extreme involvement of the participants with
their rituals, which caused them to ignore completely the
presence of the film-makers.

Luc de Heusch, in a survey of ethnographical and
sociological films, says,

> Reportages which describe authentically reli-
> gious rites fall into a special category. In these
> cases, the fervour, the contemplation or the mystic
> frenzy of the participants enables the camera to
> insinuate itself into the heart of the religious phe-
> nomenon without affecting it. [5]

Rouch became so adept at using his camera effectively
in these situations that Edgar Morin, another sociologist, defined him as a "diver film-maker" because of his skill in
diving down into the real environment.

One of his best films of this type was Les Maitres Fous ("The Manic Priests"), made in 1954 during a visit to Ghana. The film portrays religious ceremonies of detribalized African groups who have failed to adapt to the life of the more sophisticated white culture.

In 1955, Rouch collected the best of his films touching on various aspects of life in French Nigerian territories into a feature-length film entitled Les Fils de l'Eau. Quoting Alain Tanner (from his article, "Recording Africa"),

> ... Feeling themselves at one with the gods that inhabit the animals and plants around them, these Africans have no desire to dominate nature, to develop the techniques of mechanical progress. Rather, their existence is a constant and willing submission to the forces of nature; and it is this mystique which forms the essential themes of Rouch's films. [6]

Because of his films on African life and customs, Rouch became more convinced than ever that the best means for studying ethnography was through film. In his own words,

> We are really on the eve of a complete revolution to be achieved by the cinema. I sincerely believe that it is impossible to describe an African or American Indian or Polynesian ceremony, in which several things are happening at once, without a film camera. In ten years' time one will no longer be able to describe a ceremony as in a book on anthropology by writing that 'the priest comes in from the right. He is dressed in blue. He is carrying a red vase in his arms. He puts it down on the ground....' The whole of that would correspond to one second on a film.... [7]

He contends that with the development of lightweight, synchronous cameras and tape recorders, everything would change in the study of African music as well as of behavior patterns. "I am almost sure that in, say 50 years' time," he says, "there won't be a single anthropological book being written to describe behavior. It will all be done with films. "[8]

Having begun his career with ethnological films of African life and customs, he became increasingly interested in applying the same methods to fictional stories, using im-

provised situations. He began to create his plots and subjects at the actual moment of filming, a general practice of
most nouvelle vague directors in France.

In 1958 Rouch made his first feature film, Moi, un
Noir ("I, a Black") on the "anxieties, the dreams and the
psychological contradictions of the new African generation. "9
This film is an objective account of the life of three Nigerian
migrants living in Treichville, the slum district of Abidjan
on the Ivory Coast. In this film, Rouch used these Africans
to portray various aspects of their lives, as well as their
dreams, and staged situations to suit his purpose.

> Three African actors relate who they are, what
> they want to be,... what they have done, their hopes
> and their disappointment. The plan of the story is
> invented by the actors ... they move in a universe
> which lies midway between wish and reality but
> which never ceases to be a faithful description of
> African urban society. 10

The film really centers around two of the men, both
of whom have adopted names for themselves: one is Edward
G. Robinson, who likes boxing and identifies himself with a
great boxer, and the other, Eddie Constantine. They "watch
themselves living and appraise themselves.... Rouch here
deliberately ventures a transfer from objective ethnographic
description" to description of subjective content of the mind. 11

The film was shot silent and, in order to give the
images an authenticity that no traditional type of narration
ever could, Rouch then asked the young stevedore who called
himself Edward G. Robinson to see the film and deliver a
commentary on the events as he saw them. His comments
were recorded and used as the narration for the film. This
pattern of including a character's comments on the film in
which he appears is one that Rouch followed in some of his
later films.

Rouch has said, "In Moi, un Noir, the actors played
their everyday existence in front of the camera. I did not
hide in order to film them. We were partners. "12

In 1960 Rouch made La Pyramide Humaine, another
film on the problem of racial conflict in Africa. His idea
was to film the lives of some Africans and European students
in the mixed Abidjan school, but he soon found that there was

no contact whatsoever between these two groups outside the
school. To overcome this difficulty he thought of a fictional
story in which the black and white students try to make contact with each other. He then asked the students to initiate
conversations and improvise reactions in certain given situations. As he put it, "I asked the students, both African and
European, girls and boys to play a kind of psychodrama about
racial relationships."[13] Here again Rouch shot the film without a sound track and post-synchronized the dialogue, but he
could not recapture the spontaneous hesitations and awkward-
ness of the students' original conversation because they had
matured during the nine months in which the film was made
and could not reproduce the true dialogue of their first meetings. However, this film is one of Rouch's most interesting
experiments using non-professionals in an artificial situation.

 After La Pyramide Humaine Rouch returned to Paris
and with Edgar Morin made Chronique d'un Eté[14] ("Chronicle
of a Summer," 1961), on the lives of some Parisians. It
was in connection with this film that the term cinéma vérité
came into being, as previously mentioned. This full-length
feature, initially 21 hours long and later cut to one hour and
forty-five minutes, was photographed in 16mm by the well-
known Canadian cinematographer, Michel Brault, and later
enlarged to 35mm for theatrical release. The film begins by
showing the reactions of passersby in Paris to the question,
"Are you happy?" and continues by interviewing people in
great detail about their work, their fears, their anxieties,
etc. Finally, one sees the film participants viewing the film
in a screening room, their reactions to the interviews, and
the subsequent discussions. Rouch states that Chronique d'un
Eté was an attempt to combine Vertov's theory and Flaherty's
method.[15]

 With the development of lightweight tape recorders at
this time Rouch was able to record the sound simultaneously
with the picture on location, thus eliminating the problem of
post-synchronization of sound that had confronted him in La
Pyramide Humaine.

 In Chronique d'un Eté, however, he encountered fresh
problems with the Parisians he was photographing. They
were not at ease in front of the camera as the Africans had
been; in fact, most of the time they were paralyzed and
could not say anything. Rouch does not analyze the reason,
but it is obvious that to the African primitives the presence
of the camera did not mean the same as it meant to the so-

phisticated Parisians. The writer has experienced such situations many times in the remote villages of the Middle East,
where farmers who had no concept of the camera acted as
naturally and spontaneously in front of it as if it had not been
there; in cosmopolitan areas, however, people often "dried
up" or were paralyzed before the camera and could not pro-
ject their natural selves.

When faced with this problem in Chronique d'un Eté
Rouch discovered that the camera is not a mere recording
apparatus but also a stimulant. People do not know some
aspects of themselves, but seem suddenly to discover new
facets of their character when facing the camera. Rouch thus
developed one of his principal theories in cinéma vérité film-
making, a theory diverging from the ideas held by some other
exponents of this style, notably Richard Leacock (the diver-
gence will be discussed in a later chapter). The best way
of explaining this theory may be to quote Jean Rouch himself:

> You push these people to confess themselves,
> and it seemed to us without any limit. Some of the
> public who saw the film said that the film was a
> film of exhibitionists. I don't think so. It is not
> exactly exhibitionism: it is a very strange kind of
> confession in front of the camera where the camera
> is, let's say, a mirror, and also a window open to
> the outside. It may be the only way out for these
> persons who have some trouble, to open this win-
> dow and to say to the other people what their trou-
> bles are. [16]

Rouch and Morin were so carried away with this film
that they went on shooting and shooting and finally ended up
(as previously stated) with 21 hours of rushes on a surfeit of
characters, all of which, according to Rouch, was "absolutely
fantastic" and could not be cut to a showable length without
loss of authenticity. In order to avoid such an enormous
amount of footage, Rouch decided (in his subsequent films) to
confine his shooting to a day or so, use a fictional story as
his theme, improvise, and not have a multiplicity of characters as he had in Chronique d'un Eté.

But he experienced the same editing problem in his
next production, La Punition[17] (shot in October, 1960 and
released in 1963), despite the fact that this feature-length
film, an experiment in improvisation, was shot over a week-
end and with only four characters. All the ingredients of

cinéma vérité--real location, improvisation by non-actors and director, etc.--were present in this fiction film. His cameraman for this film was Michel Brault, a pioneer in cinéma vérité in Canada, famous for his hand-held camera work, and the photographer for Chronique d'un Eté. Rouch pays him tribute:

> It was Brault who brought us new shooting techniques, which we didn't know and which we have been copying ever since.... We have to admit that everything we have done in French cinéma vérité derives from the Canadian National Film Board.[18]

The story of La Punition concerns a girl, Nadine Ballot (from Rouch's La Pyramide Humaine), who for one day is thrown out of the school where she is studying philosophy. Afraid of going home, she wanders around in Paris and meets three men--a student, a Negro and a middle-aged engineer, "who represent, roughly, love, adventure and money."[19] The student declares himself to be in love with her and then leaves her with the middle-aged engineer; he asks her to come home with him and his Negro acquaintance. The actors have no written text, but between takes (lasting ten minutes) a general pattern was laid out for them by Rouch. They were even their own sound recordists; Rouch had Nadine carry around a satchel with a tape recorder concealed in it, and miniature microphones were supplied to all four characters.

In spite of his resolution to limit initial footage on this film, Rouch ended up with six hours of rushes, all of which had some points of interest and proved extremely difficult to cut to a showable length. He blamed Brault for some of this: his superb camera work often made editing impossible. Because Brault was an expert in camera movement, when he began to move there was nothing that could be cut. When from sheer exhaustion he was forced to sit and photograph, it became possible to edit the film.[20]

When La Punition was finally edited, the entire character emphasis was changed. As Rouch remarks, "In the rushes the student was absolutely wonderful and the engineer was ridiculous. When the film was edited, the student was ridiculous and the engineer was wonderful!"[21] So what is the solution to the cutting of this style of film? Rouch, while admitting that the rules are still not known and that one is still hampered with inadequate technical means, offers two temporary solutions. One is to show the complete rushes unedited because the moment one tries to condense them into a commercial length something is lost. He rests his theory on the premise that when one piece of film (a fact) is joined to another piece of film (another fact), a third phenomenon is produced--contrary to the aim of cinéma vérité, which is to present the unadulterated truth. For this reason Rouch believes that the entire 21-hour rushes of Chronique d'un Eté should have been shown because the edited version lost the whole concept he was after. He complains:

> We are taking elements of reality and cutting them by rules which are at the time mere arbitrary whims which make us think that some elements are too long, we don't know why.
>
> ... when we cut this type of material, a scissors-cut thrusts everything before and after it into space. So we have to rethink the film completely. This is why editing takes so long and gets so difficult. [22]

Then he poses the question, "Will the solution be to go along to this kind of film without editing at all, and play the whole thing 'directly' like live T.V.?"[23] In this respect Rouch's concept of cinéma vérité differs drastically from Vertov's Kino-Pravda. Vertov says:

> If one records on film everything that man has seen one will naturally get only a jumbled mess. If one edits scientifically, the things that were photographed become clearer. If you throw out whatever bothers you, better still. We will thus be able to gain an organized memory of impressions from an ordinary eye. [24]

Rouch's other solution, which seems to be more practical, is to be one's own cameraman and cut the film in the camera, thus resolving the problem of subsequent editing. He pointed out that film-makers were still slaves regarding sound and could not effectively cut while shooting sync-sound until the necessary technical means were available. With the recent technological breakthroughs that have taken place in motion picture equipment, and in particular the utilization of crystal components in cameras and tape recorders, most of such problems have been resolved.

Rouch was more pleased with the edited version of

La Punition than with Chronique d'un Eté, having had less
footage to cope with, and commented that the best part of the
film is the edited portion. In short, Rouch sees two ways
open to him:

> First: the choice of a subject limited in time
> so that the rushes would not last more than, say,
> a day.... Second: to have a film in which the
> author is conscious of what he is filming at every
> instant, and only presses the camera button to
> film something which fits exactly into the film he
> wants to make. [25]

Rouch was well satisfied with the dialogue in La Punition, not only because at this time he had better and more
manageable sound equipment to use, but also because his
characters spoke in an everyday conversational manner. He
said, "What I really like in this film is the banality of the
dialogue. Because it is like that, that one speaks in life.
I would like to better use this procedure in order to fabri-
cate films of fiction."[26] He continued, "Take any film you
like with dialogue by Jeanson or Prévert and the dialogue is
quite unreal: people never stammer ... or make bitter retorts,
and so forth. I admit it's a perfect piece of artistic reconstruction; but it never exists in real life."[27]

From La Punition Rouch learned something else about
this kind of film-making--that he could make fiction from
reality:

> Personally, I thought that La Punition was
> primarily an experience of passion. Whether the
> film flopped or succeeded was a small matter. The
> important thing which we now know is that we can
> manufacture fiction from reality. Save for the
> fact that we don't yet know the rules and I am still
> a bit of a sorcerer's apprentice. [28]

The film, in fact, pleased virtually nobody and was a failure
for both Rouch and the public alike. Nadine, the main
character, portrayed a role which was not really herself;
she had to improvise on a theme which was not natural to
her, and she did not seem to be involved in the film. When
it was shown at the UNESCO Club in Paris in 1963, it elic-
ited great criticism, particularly from Roberto Rossellini,
one of the harshest critics of cinéma vérité, who, as stated
in Chapter I, believes that this method of filming is useful

only for collecting scientific documentation. Rouch himself admitted that La Punition was "not a film but an attempt to create fiction out of reality, to make something marvelous with the banal. "[29]

In 1963 Rouch made a film in Montreal for the Film Board of Canada entitled Rose et Landry. This film is about an African who is caught between his acquired French culture and his vanishing native tradition which he is forgetting. Louis Marcorelles, reviewing the film for Cahiers du Cinéma, wrote,

> Without speeches or sermons, Rouch makes us become conscious without our being aware of it, that what for us is the best, the only possible world, could have the exact opposite meaning for those people who belong to another and different civilization. Objective and subjective at the same time, he proposes that we should feel inside a state of being, a spiritual climate different from our own. [30]

The film opens with Landry and his friend Rose dancing the twist in a night club in Abidjan. Marcorelles points out that

> ... while copying the steps, partaking of the sophisticated pleasures of the whites, they do not reject for all that their natural heritage ... Rose can carry an urn on her head just like the women of Abidjan. Landry admires his mother and venerates his grandmother who taught him the elements of witchcraft. [31]

Rouch made two other short films in 1964: Les Veuves de Quinze Ans and the episode "Gare du Nord" in Paris Vu Par, the latter being an interesting answer to his perennial problem of editing. This film is the story of a woman who quarrels with her husband and runs out of the house, where she meets a stranger who commits suicide when she refuses to go away with him. The film is 20 minutes long and consists of only two takes.

> Rouch's later films are experimental works that aim to recreate the cinema from scratch. Starting from the discovery of the catalytic force of the camera in bringing people to reveal their

> true selves, Rouch has gone on to examine the pos-
> sibilities of fusing fiction and reality by improvisa-
> tion and spontaneous shooting. [32]

Hampered financially by his lack of commercial success in cinéma vérité, Rouch returned to documentary filming
in Abidjan, where he found the Africans so easy to photograph.
However, in these films he shows a style moving away from
pure documentary and into a form of film-making much more
complex and exciting. Switching from technology, as a civil
engineer, to anthropology and then films, he exhibits within
this medium of expression a melange of ethnography, sociology, and group therapy. By allowing his characters the last
word, as in Moi, un Noir and some of his other films discussed above, he shows his awareness of the moral implica-
tions of filming people's intimate revelations. But his main
concern with cinéma vérité remained that of building fiction
with reality, using non-actors and improvised techniques.
Rouch was never interested in preconceived stories for his
films in cinéma vérité style, as some other French practitioners were. In his opinion the ideal would be to make a
cinema of improvised fiction. He states: "The cinema of
improvised fiction, in my view, is a cinema in which we
guide elemental reality and where we write the story while
we are actually shooting. "[33]

In the course of his film-making, Rouch discovered
(or rediscovered) patterns of behavior in given situations
that are deeply revealing of human nature. At one time he
wrote about an experience he had during the filming of Je
Suis la Président de la République, which dealt with the basic
fact that the President of the Nigerian Republic was--after
all--just a man like any other. One day while Rouch was
filming the President in deep conversation with a young
Nigerian student, as they strolled together through the Lux-
embourg Gardens in Paris, he was reminded of the fact that
"one's gait takes the same rhythm as one's thought" and that
one's thoughts are directly affected by his immediate environment. He says,

> ... he [the President] was influenced by the autumn
> landscape of that garden and suddenly the sun went
> behind a cloud. We continued shooting and there
> all of a sudden he began to talk about war, for the
> garden had become sad. But when the sun came
> out again he said, 'Let's talk about more pleasant
> things.' There we saw a complete adhesion be-

tween landscape, decor, movement and thought. [34]

Rouch also used this example to point up the fact that what was recorded simultaneously that day could "never have been given by the sound alone, the image alone, or the written word. "

As might be expected (because of his avant-garde ideas and techniques), Rouch did not escape the criticism of his contemporaries. Jean-Louis Bory wrote a critical review of the films discussed here and the title of his article reflects the author's attitude: "Vessies et Lanternes" ("The Moon Is Not Made of Green Cheese"). Although he had great admiration for Rouch as a scholar, ethnographer and cinematographer, he freely pointed out what he considered to be weaknesses in the film-maker's approach. For instance, he commented that Rouch's characters "become objects of experiment, let themselves be manipulated like objects" and his "camera not only spies, but it provokes the transformation in order to shoot it. The camera vérité of Rouch not only tracks the reality; it uses it. "

He adds, "The truth of his cinéma vérité belongs less to the truth of a reporter than to the theatrical truth. " Then he ends his criticism by saying, "... Rouch is directing, from movie to movie, less as a scientific investigator than as the poet of the love of men. "[35]

That, of course, is one man's opinion. How different from that of the film-maker himself, who--as has been stated above--considered characters in his films as "partners" rather than objects to be manipulated!

Peter Graham criticizes another aspect of Rouch's techniques in an article written for Film Quarterly:

> If film is art, its purpose is not merely to record, but to select, organize, and alchemize what is recorded. Watching the material that Rouch and Ruspoli collected, in spite of its undeniable interest, is like being allowed to see only the palette of a painter who is producing a masterpiece; it has all the elements that could go to make a work of art, but it is never more than a tantalizing suggestion of what one might have seen. [36]

Rouch agrees that in cinema total objectivity is impos-

sible, because the moment one aims the camera at something
or somebody a subjective choice has been made. But he
believes that, despite this inherent choice of what to film, a
high degree of dispassionate objectivity can still be achieved.
Cinema for Rouch is an instrument of communication, initially among those involved in making it and then between the
film and the audience. He believes that it is a question of
throwing light on truth which is hidden from us by the particular prejudices and social values and conventions of our
time. Rouch's main approach to cinéma vérité is to place
his characters in a situation with dramatic possibilities, let
them improvise, and then film them. He states, "If these
people have something to say, and if I am clever enough to
put them in a situation with dramatic possibilities, that is
when something uniquely valuable can happen."[37]

NOTES

[1]The other two are Dziga Vertov and Cartier-Bresson.

[2]Ian Cameron and Mark Shivas, "Interviews," Movie,
No. 8 (April, 1963), p. 22 (Interview with Jean Rouch).

[3]Herbert G. Luft, "Karl Freund," Films in Review,
XIV, No. 2 (February, 1963), p. 93.

[4]Cameron and Shivas, loc. cit.

[5]Luc de Heusch, "The Cinema and Social Science: A
Survey of Ethnographic and Sociological Films,"
U.N.E.S.C.O., No. 16, 1962, p. 32.

[6]Alain Tanner, "Recording Africa," Sight and Sound,
Vol. 26, No. 1 (Summer, 1956), p. 42.

[7]Cameron and Shivas, op. cit., p. 23.

[8]Ibid.

[9]Luc de Heusch, op. cit., p. 50.

[10]Ibid.

[11]Ibid.

[12]Ibid.

[13]Cameron and Shivas, op. cit., p. 22

[14]16mm, B and W, feature length. Camera: Coutant-Mathot KMT. Recorders: Nagra Neo-Pilot and Perfectone. Synchronization system: Pilot-guided. Photographed by Michel Brault, Roger Morillère, Raoul Coutard, Jean-Jacques Tarbes. Edited by Jean Ravel, Nina Baratier, Françoise Colin. Directed by Jean Rouch, Edgar Morin. Won "Prix de la Critique" at the 1961 Cannes Festival.

[15]"Table Ronde: Festival de Tours en Collaboration avec l'U. N. E. S. C. O. " Image et Son, No. 160 (Mars, 1963), p. 6.

[16]Cameron and Shivas, loc. cit.

[17]16mm, B and W, feature length. Camera: Coutant-Mathot KMT. Photographed by Michel Brault, Roger Morillère, George Dufaux. Directed by Jean Rouch. Players: Nadine Ballot, Jean-Marc Simon, Jean-Claude Darnel, Modeste Landry.

[18]Eric Rohmer et Louis Marcorelles, "Entretien avec Jean Rouch, " Cahiers du Cinéma, XXIV, No. 144 (Juin, 1963), p. 17.

[19]Roy Armes, French Cinema Since 1946, Vol. II: The Personal Style (Amsterdam: Drukkerijen vh. , Ellerman Harms NV, 1966), p. 128.

[20]Rohmer et Marcorelles, op. cit., p. 7.

[21]Cameron and Shivas, loc. cit.

[22]Rohmer et Marcorelles, op. cit., pp. 6-7.

[23]Ibid. , p. 7.

[24]Dziga Vertov, "Dziga Vertov--Kinoks-Revolution II, " Cahiers du Cinéma, XXV, No. 146 (Août, 1963), p. 19.

[25]Cameron and Shivas, op. cit., p. 23.

[26]Rohmer et Marcorelles, op. cit., p. 5.

[27]Ibid.

[28]Ibid. , p. 6.

[29]Armes, op. cit. , p. 129.

[30]Louis Marcorelles, "Truth Fair," Cahiers du Cinéma, Vol. XXIV, No. 140 (February, 1963), p. 32.

[31]Ibid.

[32]Armes, loc. cit.

[33]Rohmer et Marcorelles, op. cit. , p. 8.

[34]"Enrico Fulchugnoni and Pierre Barbin, Editors, debate among major delegates to Tours Festival, 1963 (for UNESCO)," Image et Son, No. 160 (Mars, 1963), p. 17.

[35]Jean-Louis Bory, "Vessies et Lanternes," Artsept No. 2, Le Cinéma et la Vérité (Avril/Juin, 1963), pp. 57-60.

[36]Peter Graham, "Cinema-Vérité in France," Film Quarterly, Vol. XVII, No. 4, (Summer, 1964), p. 31.

[37]Rohmer et Marcorelles, op. cit. , p. 10.

CHAPTER IX

RICHARD LEACOCK: THE AMERICAN SCHOOL

      Richard Leacock, whose work in cinéma vérité may
well represent the American School of this movement, is
said to be a born film-maker. He says of himself, "At the
age of eight I had scarcely seen even two films, but I knew
then that I wanted to make movies."[1] He was born in 1921
in the Canary Islands, and was raised in England. As a
child he was given very little opportunity to see films. When
he was 11, however, he saw the Russian documentary Turksib (1929, Victor Turin), which influenced him greatly.

      In 1934 his father bought him a camera and he made
his first film in the Canary Islands, where his father owned
a large banana plantation. Leacock recalls:

> It was a 16mm idiot-film about the Canary
> bananas done in the manner of Turksib.... A
> particular thing about the film still strikes me to-
> day: I neglected to film people. I filmed people
> then only when they were going about their business
> of packing bananas or digging trenches. Taking
> people at their work seemed more obvious to me;
> contrariwise, I found it silly to photograph static
> faces, to make portraits, as all others encourage
> one to do. [2]

      At this time young Richard was attending Darbington
Hall School. His geography teacher encouraged his love of
cinema and together they made a number of instructional
films for geography and a few about the school. It so happened that Monica, Robert Flaherty's daughter, also was en-
rolled there. Flaherty, who was making The Man of Aran
at the time, saw young Richard's film about the Canary Islands and, although he did not particularly like the film itself,
he was delighted with the idea that a 13-year-old could make

one.   Flaherty told Leacock, "One day we'll make a film together."[3] And many years later they did.

Leacock went on to Harvard to study physics--not to
become a physicist, but rather to become a film-maker.   In
his own words, "I did not choose this field because I wanted
to become a physicist, I wanted to make films."[4]   Then
came the war and he was sent to Burma and China as an
Army combat photographer to make newsreels.   After the
war Leacock was "free." He relates:

> I had no idea if I could get any kind of position.
> So, I visited Flaherty and he was pleased.   He
> didn't want to discuss what I had done, wanted to
> see no film, didn't want to test me in any way.
> He asked me only, 'Are you free?' I said, 'Yes.'
> And he said, 'O.K. We are going to Louisiana.'
> Just like that: bang, on the basis of a small ba-
> nana film.[5]

They made Louisiana Story (1948) together, Flaherty
directing and Leacock photographing.   Both of them sought
to portray reality, but they had problems in shooting sync-
sound and capturing the true event.   Leacock comments:

> Already when we were working on Louisiana
> Story, I saw that when we were using small cam-
> eras, we had tremendous flexibility, we could do
> anything we wanted, and get a wonderful sense of
> cinema.   The moment we had to shoot dialogue,
> lip-synch--everything had to be locked down, the
> whole nature of the film changed.... We could no
> longer watch things as they developed; we had to
> impose ourselves to such an extent upon everything
> that happened before us, that everything sort of
> died.   And this problem kept coming up with me,
> sometimes making me absolutely furious.[6]

Like many of his contemporaries, Leacock was seeking freedom from the impedimenta of ungainly equipment in
order to capture reality spontaneously and give the film life.
As a result of his work with Flaherty he rejected all the
Hollywood types of artifice, convention and decor.   The
Hollywood stars, he maintained, portrayed a life that bore
no relation to the lives and actions of real people.

During the period following the making of Louisiana

Story, Leacock made some minor films, edited others, and in general gained experience in the various phases of film-making. In 1954 he was given a chance to make a film by himself, one he refers to as his "first film." The film, entitled Toby, was made for the Omnibus Television Company. It is a journalistic report of a real event--the performance of a play in a tent show in the Midwest. Although using conventional, cumbersome equipment for this film (35mm Mitchell cameras and sound recorders), because of the recurrent nature of the subject Leacock managed to photograph a little bit of the play each night and came out with a film that pleased him. In spite of the immobility of equipment, he managed to capture the true feeling of what actually happened. When the film was shown on television, Robert Drew, a photographer-reporter for Time-Life, Inc., saw it and called Leacock. At the time, Drew was in the process of trying to employ sync-sound in film journalism at Harvard. Leacock reports:

> ... [Drew] had become obsessed with a theory that he had developed on his own, a feeling that journalism and television weren't doing justice to each other.... He had seen the show by accident, called me up, came down to New York and this marvelous thing happened. Somebody you had never heard of in your life came in and had understood every single thing in the film. And more than understood it, had projected from it. [7]

Drew and Leacock soon found that their thinking ran parallel. Drew's concepts stemmed from journalism; Leacock's from cinema. Drew wanted to report not only what was going on in any given situation, but also to give people the feeling of being right on the scene. Their philosophy was to use the camera not as a participant in film-making to dictate and change the scene for its own benefit, but rather as a neutral bystander to report the truth as it was revealed before it. Bernard Dort calls it "descriptive camera" and says the use of the descriptive camera should no longer "dramatize or even tell us a story; its sole function will be to reveal the true world of life to us--without ever presuming to judge it." [8]

Drew and Leacock called their approach "Living Camera." "Living Camera" meant to them that the film-maker captures not only the facts of a situation (for facts can be distorted by the unscrupulous or careless cameraman or editor) but the whole feeling or essence of what is happening as the film-maker sees it. At the time, both men wanted to achieve reportage not only in the television sense of "this is the way it happened," but also reportage through which the film-maker could convey to the audience a feeling of being right on the scene and sharing the experience with him.

Drew, however, was more interested in expressing a kind of emotional truth rather than the intellectual truth which current television journalism tries to present.[9] His principal method, according to William Bleum, was:

> ... preserving an essential reality by eliminating the subject's awareness of the camera and ... eliciting emotional response from the viewer by making the camera an active participant in the events recorded.[10]

Louis Marcorelles writes that discussions with Leacock and his associates convinced him that the aim of cinéma vérité (according to them) is to "find out the essential in a being, those moments of abandon when the individual is too tired or too relaxed, and does not take care to protect himself from others' scrutiny"--a concept manifested by Dziga Vertov, as discussed in Chapter II. Later in his article Marcorelles says, "The Drew-Leacock method poses as a premise, a frantic search for the truth, in a certain sense, the will to drive the secret movement of beings out into the open, while avoiding any 'sensationalism.'"[11] That is-- discovering internal movement by studying external movement!

Drew and Leacock decided to unite in order to create a new form of journalism for television, but the same old problems plagued them. Before their collaboration, Leacock had made a film on Leonard Bernstein's visit to Israel, using a 16mm camera for the first time. But the film did not turn out the way he had envisioned. Bulkiness of equipment, especially sound equipment, was a great drawback in achieving the kind of film he was after. He became determined to develop equipment that would make such attempts more feasible and successful.

Inspired by an electronic watch Leacock had seen, he and Drew joined forces with the Maysles brothers, Donn Alan Pennebaker, Gregory Shuker and others, with financial backing from Time, Inc., and began developing equipment for this kind of cinematography.

Meanwhile, they made a film on Cuba (Cuba Si, Yanki No, 1960), then one in Spain on bullfighting, and a feature-length documentary on football. Their modified equipment did not function as easily as they wished, but with each attempt to use it they learned something new and continued improving it. Their goal was to be able to photograph, remaining as inconspicuous as they could within a situation where something dynamic was happening, and for this purpose they needed light and mobile equipment to record sight and sound synchronously.

The first time their equipment was sufficiently developed to be completely mobile, enabling them to go into a situation and photograph and record the sound with ease, was in 1960 when they made their famous film Primary. Luc de Heusch, referring to the new equipment used in filming Primary, said, "Thanks to this highly mobile technique of the 'open sesame' camera, the producers succeeded in filming in the most 'candid' fashion."[12] The film is a candid study of Senators John Kennedy and Hubert Humphrey in their now historic contest in the Wisconsin primary election.

Leacock calls Primary basically a reportage film. Nevertheless, it is a dynamic, exciting story and has a certain natural structure of its own. Albert Maysles paid tribute to it by saying, "I know damn well that people will see PRIMARY one hundred years from now."[13]

Leacock's idea was to follow Kennedy during the campaign, using their newly-developed equipment and photographing what went on without intruding on the scene. Drew and Leacock approached Kennedy, and Leacock recalls:

> At first he thought it was a crazy idea; then he asked me, 'How do I know you won't make me out to look like a fool?' I explained to him that only one person would be in the room, that all would run quietly, without tripod, and we wanted only to observe. I told him he could take my word as a gentleman. He thought for a moment and then said, 'Okay.'[14]

Al Maysles and Leacock shot the picture, and Drew and Pennebaker handled the sound. This was their first breakthrough. At last they were able to walk in and out of buildings, up and down stairs, film in a taxi or in an office-- in any place, and get synchronized sound and pictures of what really happened. Their equipment included a modified 16mm Auricon and a Nagra tape recorder--each running in synchronization by means of a Bulova Accutron electronic watch system. With this equipment, which was small and portable enough not to intrude by noise or appearance, Leacock and his colleagues photographed Kennedy and Humphrey with very little difficulty. Two teams, each consisting of a cameraman and a sound-man, followed the two candidates continually and photographed some remarkably revealing glimpses of them, their wives and their entourage, without interfering with their activities.

When the filming was completed, all the crew members worked together and in four weeks' time edited the 18,000 feet of film down to 2,000 feet (about 55 minutes long). The experiment was an astonishing feat and proved to be what they were after in film-making: it worked.

It should be noted, however, that in cinéma vérité (or as Drew and Leacock called it, "Living Camera"), having portable sync-sound equipment is by no means the only consideration. The attitude of the subject being photographed toward the film-maker is of utmost importance. If the filmmaker is not regarded as an interloper, then the subject may forget his presence and behave naturally. Pennebaker explains:

> Had Kennedy felt that Ricky [Leacock] was in any way an intruder, in a physical or moral sense, if he'd felt differently, he wouldn't have allowed certain things to happen, or he wouldn't have acted himself in the natural way he did. What actually Ricky did put into the situation was a sort of ease, so that people in the situation did not feel impelled to be directed by him, they forgot about him, in a sense. It was Ricky's moral attitude that affected their attitude to us during the shooting. [15]

Primary, a film strongly Vertovian in character and highly objective in its treatment, is an outstanding reportage film which avoids propaganda of any kind, draws no moral and follows no "plot" other than the chronology of the events which led to Kennedy's winning the election.

During the making of Primary, Drew and Leacock admittedly always hoped for dramatic situations but they completely avoided asking anybody to follow specific instructions in order to achieve them.

Unfortunately, as William Bleum has said, "... the climactic moments in men's lives do not happen at the convenience of cameramen and sound-men, however unobtrusively they may wait. A dramatic situation must not only exist, but it must be approaching some definite climax when the producers arrive to record it."[16]

Claude Julien, in his article, "A Man in a Crowd," graphically compares the impact and effectiveness of the film, Primary, and Theodore W. White's book, The Making of a President (1960). He concluded that the book says things that the movie cannot (for instance, information about Republican candidates the winner of this primary would face later). He says, "Although Primary is one of the best cinéma vérité films, the author believes that White captured more accurately the facts and the 'feelings' on the written page."[17]

Carrying out their theory of the "Living Camera" approach, Drew and Leacock inaugurated a series bearing that title. Released in syndication, the series of films consisted of ten programs, each dealing with a special day, week, or month in the lives of people--all of them experiencing some crisis. The series was described as "unscripted, unrehearsed.... For the first time, the camera is a man. It sees, it hears, it moves like a man." A brochure proclaimed that "the Living Camera truly enters into the life of its subjects and lays bare, layer by layer, their character under stress."[18]

Perhaps the most memorable of their films are: The Children Were Watching (about an attempt to integrate the public schools in New Orleans), 1960; Pete and Johnnie (portraying a Negro social worker and the leader of a Puerto Rico gang in Harlem), 1961; Eddie Sachs at Indianapolis (showing a famous racing driver preparing for the big Speedway event), 1961; The Chair (showing a lawyer's desperate struggle to reprieve from execution a Negro committed for murder several years previously, but who had become a new man in prison), 1963; and Jane (about Jane Fonda's preparation for opening night of a play that eventually folded), 1963.

James Blue, writing on the cinéma vérité director's efforts to capture Truth, said, "Something close to a modern religion was born.... In the mystique of his quest ... the film maker subjugates himself to the world around him. He says to Nature, 'Not my will but thine be done.'"[19] He

says that if "Truth" is the God of this religion, then "Authenticity" is its prophet. He continued, "'Authenticity' permits
life to reveal its own truth, its own poetry, free from the
tyranny of dramatic probability."[20] In an interview with Blue
on this subject, Albert Maysles remarked, "The funny thing
is you are not at odds with the way God or Nature puts
things. You're not at odds, it's not a fight against it, but
it's harmony between you and the world."[21]

However, if the harmony that Mr. Maysles talks about
or the dramatic possibility that Mr. Bleum mentions is not
naturally inherent in a cinéma vérité story, or if the subject
is not involved in a situation which is more important to him
than the presence of the equipment and the film-maker, the
photography of all the illuminating moments of truth will not
turn into a successful, satisfying film.

In The Chair (1962),[22] considered to be one of the
best examples of the American contribution to cinéma vérité,
such factors were present. The film has a ready-made,
dramatic structure, and its protagonist is a human being so
totally involved in a life and death struggle that he is almost
unaware of the presence of the camera and the film-maker.

The story concerns the desperate struggle of a Chicago
lawyer, Donald Page Moore, to save his client, Paul Crump,
from execution in the electric chair, which is scheduled within the week. Crump is a black man, condemned to death
nine years previously for having been involved in an armed
attack in which a man had died. According to all those who
had been close to Crump during those years since his arrest,
the man had changed completely, and had been rehabilitated
to the point where all felt he could again take an honorable
place in society. The film portrays the tension and terrible
suspense in the court as the lawyer strives to convince the
jury to commute the sentence and turn Crump over to the
mercy of the Governor of Illinois. Hanging in mid-air is
the question, "Will the Governor acquiesce?"

The life of the condemned man during the five days
before his execution date, the anguish of the executioner who
is his friend, the lawyer's efforts and the court in session
are captured in the film. Finally, the Governor commutes
the sentence to life imprisonment. A thrilling moment in
the film occurs when Crump's lawyer hears the news on the
telephone and bursts into tears--an emotional scene no actor
could possibly recreate "truthfully."

The Chair works well as a cinéma vérité film because it has a structure and a natural drama, based on actual events.

Armando Plebe, writing about the necessity of structure for such films, says:

> A form can only be cinematographically convincing if it possesses a structure, conceived through images which hold it together; in other words, the images are woven together in an organic fashion, with a beginning, a development and an end that are coherent, and above all visually coherent.... 'The Chair' by R. Leacock holds the spectator's attention through [its] able and convincing structure. [23]

The successful element of the structure in The Chair is that it has a built-in climax: Paul Crump will or will not be reprieved. Thus, it nicely fits Leacock's definition of the requirements for a subject for his "Living Camera" films:

> A film about a person who is interesting, who is involved in a situation which he cares about deeply, which comes to a conclusion within a limited period of time, where we have access to what goes on--we can be there, in other words.... [24]

Leacock and Drew spent the five days with the defense lawyer, Donald Page Moore. Gregor Shuker, who had the primary responsibility for the film, together with Donn Alan Pennebaker, covered Paul Crump and Louis Nizer, the lawyer who came in from New York to assist in the case. They all covered the hearing together. Uncertain as to how the case would turn out and, therefore, of what was important, particularly in editing, they shot 70,000 feet of film. Leacock claims that in editing they had to cut out many interesting things in order to fit the conception required of the film. But Leacock also believes that while many interesting discoveries are made by the film-maker as he photographs, more discoveries are made during the editing. For example, during the photographing of The Chair, Leacock did not particularly like Louis Nizer; but during the editing he came to have great respect for him.

Speaking about Drew Associates' films, Bleum comments:

Of these, none carried a greater significance--
a more definite finality--than 'The Chair. '
In 'The Chair' Drew's film-makers found all
the eternal elements of the great courtroom drama
clearly set in motion, with an inevitable crisis
impending. [25]

Louis Marcorelles, regarding the climax of this film,
says, "The camera here seems at one with its subject, and
the result is one of those lyrical bursts of feeling which only
the cinema can capture with just this degree of intensity."[26]

Another one of the Drew Associates' films (of the
"Living Camera" series) which again fits Leacock's definition
of an ideal subject is Eddie Sachs (originally called On the
Pole, 1962). It is the story of racing car champion Eddie
Sachs, his goals, ambitions, and style of life. The camera
follows him over a period of three consecutive years as he
seeks to win the race at the famous Indianpolis Speedway.
For the third time running, he is favored to win in 1961, but
through unexpected circumstances fails to do so, and comes
in second. The film starts with black and white footage and
then switches to color. It gives a fascinating glimpse of the
charged atmosphere of American sport and the ways of American sportsmen. Its outstanding aspects are the richness of
the live sound and the moments of genuine excitement and
suspense resulting from actual occurrences.

Because of the turn of events, what Leacock and his
associates expected to be a reportage film turned out to be
something more ambitious. They found that what happened
to the famous racing driver had all the elements of a classical drama. Leacock, in an interview, said, "We began to
realize ... that just as the theatrical sense of drama stems
from reality, people in real situations will produce drama if
we're smart enough to be able to capture it ... [without our]
asking anybody to do anything."[27]

In a cinéma vérité filming situation, Leacock said,
there are no distracting lights, no cables, no tripods, and
the camera is silent. There are only two people present:
the cameraman and the sound-man--two human beings, rather
than two technicians.

These people work ... in a delicate relationship with the person whom they are filming, who
is involved in doing something that is more im-

portant to him than the fact that we are filming
him. Instead of worrying about what we're seeing
or something, he has to do what he has to do because it's so damned important. At the moment
we can deal with intense situations, but we have
greater difficulty dealing with less intense situations. [28]

Jonas Mekas calls Eddie Sachs a documentary drama.
"We follow the protagonist, we live with him, we get to know
him, we identify with him. But we know all the time that
he is not acting his life for the camera ... the camera is
only a stranger, catching unobtrusively glimpses from his
life. "[29]

He pays tribute to Leacock: "It is not at all surprising, therefore, that the Nouvelle Vague directors, more
author-conscious than Hollywood, have been the first ones to
invade Leacock's 43rd Street studio to get acquainted with the
new techniques. Leacock's studio ... has become a sort of
crossroad of the world for the new cinema. "[30]

The film Jane (1963), also one of the Drew Associates'
films of the "Living Camera" series, did not create quite the
same sensation as Eddie Sachs and The Chair, but it is
nevertheless an important effort.

The film portrays Jane Fonda rehearsing her role in
a play in a New York theater, then leaving on tour for Philadelphia, Wilmington and Boston previous to the Broadway
premiere. The vehicle in which she is cast is an ill-fated
comedy, The Fun Couple, directed by her fiancé, Andreas.
The play is a failure and the Associates film a meeting of
the actors, director, technicians and crew, at which the
causes of the production's disastrous reception are discussed.
The agonizing decision to give up and close that very evening
is finally reached. All the facets of American show business
are there--not all of them complimentary to the industry.

The film did not fit the framework of a successful
cinéma vérité film because it lacked the kind of dramatic and
structural elements that were inherent in The Chair and Eddie
Sachs.

In Nehru (1962), unlike Primary, the "Living Camera"
is not very successful either, because the film-makers, un-
familiar with the Indian culture and election processes, did

not discover the drama they expected. The film shows 15 days in the life of Jawaharlal Nehru, the late Prime Minister of India, during the Indian elections.

Drew, Leacock and Shuker made the film, thinking that Nehru would be so highly involved in the forthcoming elections that they would end up with a film containing the kind of drama that they had found in Primary. But for Nehru the elections were such a foregone conclusion that he went about his daily routine, far removed from the high tension which Leacock, Drew and Shuker expected to find in a candidate. They continued filming him without any intrusion, as was their practice in all such ventures, without anything dramatic happening. But one day Shuker asked Nehru a leading question during the filming and Nehru's reply produced the only climax of the film. Later, in the editing (which took almost a year), they found that the only possible catalyst of the film was the question sequence.

Leacock, explaining why Nehru did not turn out to be as successful as Primary, and in support of his definition of a good "Living Camera" film, said,

> He [Nehru] wasn't involved in anything that came to a conclusion. He was just doing what he usually does day after day after day. I guess our feeling is that at the moment we're very young. We do need high-pressure situations. As we get smarter and as our equipment gets better, as we learn more about this kind of film-making, we will be able to go into situations that are less and less pressure situations. [31]

Happy Mother's Day (formerly called The Fischer Quintuplets, 1963-64)[32] is another of the Drew Associates' films which provides an excellent example of editing in cinéma vérité films. Leacock believes that a cinéma vérité film must be edited by the cameraman himself. He contends that the cinematographer is the only one who can understand the particular aspect of reality he intended to capture in a given situation, and the only one who can re-establish the feeling of this reality through editing.

The film on the quintuplets was made for the American Broadcasting Company by Drew Associates. Due to legal complications, they had to give the network two prints of everything shot, from which ABC edited a half-hour film for

showing on television. Leacock and his associates, who
photographed the quintuplets, then edited their own version.
In an interview with James Blue, Leacock says:

> ... you cannot imagine two more different films.
> Now the ABC film is all perfectly 'true.' It's just
> uninteresting. They are not distorting except by
> omission. They simply were not aware of what
> was going on. They didn't see it in the material.
> It just became a mish-mash about sweet little chil-
> dren lying in cradles and girls singing songs and
> murses telling you in interviews how the babies
> were born and all that sort of stuff. All of which
> was 'true' and perfectly fine. It just missed what
> I found significant. [33]

Happy Mother's Day, portraying events surrounding the
birth of the Fischer quintuplets in Aberdeen, South Dakota,
is, as Patricia Jaffe says, "a real American document in
the best Sinclair Lewis tradition. When the Chamber of
Commerce and the Ladies Auxiliary ... move into action to
exploit the commercial possibilities of the blessed event,
Leacock's searching probing camera almost unwittingly lays
bare the soul of American commercialism."[34]

Leacock recognized the significance of the social and
economic problems thrust upon the modest-income family
with five children when, suddenly doubling that number, they
were forced to sacrifice their privacy to commercial exploitation to pay their bills. The film captures the almost tragic
complications that the birth of the quintuplets imposed on the
Fischer family.

Unlike Rouch, who believes the presence of the camera
modifies the action, Leacock claims that it does not really
affect the people who are being filmed, depending, of course,
on the intensity of the situation they are in, as well as the
nature of the person filming it.

> ... if we walk in on Mrs. Fischer, the mother of
> the quintuplets, alone when she is doing nothing,
> we are the only interesting thing in the room, so
> we change it enormously. But if we walk in on
> Mrs. Fischer when she is trying to get the kids
> off to school and she's mad as a hornet at them
> because they're late or something--then we change
> it very little.... We are really only successful

in finding out anything when we are filming somebody who is more concerned with what he is doing
than with the fact that we are filming him. [35]

An incident occurred during the filming of Happy
Mother's Day that illustrates Leacock's belief that the "essence" of an event cannot be recaptured if restaged. Two
children run out into the street to see the approaching
Fischer parade; when they get scared, they retreat to the
curb. The sequence lends excitement and "anticipation" to
the film. Leacock says that should the photographer have
missed the incident and asked the children to do it again,
all the feeling of true excitement would have been lost. He
believes that the minute the film-maker starts intervening in
any way, people will stop being themselves and the whole
feeling of reality will disappear.

Another incident that occurred during the filming of
the quints' story proves his point. He states:

> At one moment I was in the radio station, and
> the guy was talking about the Quints and the secre-
> tary suddenly stuck her head in the door and said,
> 'Senator So-and-So is on the line from Washington.'
> And he reacted and something happened, I don't
> know, I ran out of film or something. And I asked
> afterwards if the secretary couldn't stick her head
> in and say it. And we cracked up laughing. The
> difference was so gigantic. It was the same girl.
> Five minutes later you ask her to do it and it was
> absolutely grotesque. And when we ran the rushes
> here we all cracked up every time we looked at it.
> It was meaningless. [36]

Patricia Jaffe pays this tribute to the film: "An extra-
ordinary film. One of the reasons Happy Mother's Day is
so good is because of the way it is put together.... When
the cameraman is really operating smoothly and moving from
one image to another with ease, the footage has the quality
and rhythm of a ballet, and whole sequences may be left
intact. "[37]

Happy Mother's Day won awards at the Leipzig and
Venice Film Festivals, and was discussed widely in European
film centers.

Leacock worked with Drew Associates until June, 1963,

when he left to set up his own company. He made other
films with Drew Associates, but a study of all of these would
be beyond the scope of this book.

Leacock's method in "Living Camera" films is to utilize two men on a team, one to photograph the picture and
the other to record the sound. When the photography is
completed, the same people will edit the film. This is why
Leacock prefers the term film-maker, rather than cameraman, sound-man, editor--because the whole process becomes
integrated. If there is more than one cameraman in a filming situation, they will all edit the picture together. In each
filming set-up, however, there must be only one crew of two
people present--the cameraman and the sound-man. During
the filming of The Chair one camera crew followed the lawyer, and one photographed Paul Crump in his cell. Both
crews, however, covered the hearings. In more complicated
situations there may be more than one camera crew, each
in a different place, as in the film Football, where eight
teams of two people each covered the event because of the
magnitude of the subject.

As the success of a cinéma vérité film is dependent
on the structure and what unfolds in the filming, occasionally
the choice of a subject for a film proves entirely unworkable.
Leacock admits that "sometimes we make mistakes, we think
we have a good idea, but at the end of a few days' work we
see nothing interesting will come about; then, we quickly
change our subject."[38]

The "Living Camera" technique, then, is dependent
upon a number of strict laws which govern its successful
use: the nature of the subject; the deep involvement of the
people in the film in something which precludes concern about
the presence of the film-makers and their equipment; a structure so that the film takes on a natural rather than an en-
forced continuity; and an unavoidable conclusion.

In a "Living Camera" style, Leacock neither asks his
subjects questions nor gives them directions* but he attempts
without intruding to gather evidence about which the viewer
can make up his own mind. The personality of the film-
maker, instead of directing the event, is completely absorbed

_____

*An exception was the question put to Nehru--and that proved
to be one of his least successful films.

in recording it in his own way. "All filming until now," Leacock says, "has been essentially an extension of the theater, where you control what's happening. Only very few people--Flaherty always comes to mind--saw the cinema not as controlling, but as observing, watching, which in a way ties up with journalism."[39] He goes on to explain that in controlled filming one can always question the end result:

> Many film-makers feel that the aim of the film-maker is to have complete control. Then the conception of what happens is limited by the conception of the film-maker. We don't want to put this limit on actuality. What's happening, the action, has no limitations, neither the significance of what's happening. The film-maker's problem is more a problem of how to convey it.[40]

A number of critics have questioned the validity of a style of film-making in which the film-maker claims that he films the "truth." By the very selection of a frame, they say, objectivity becomes subjective and one shows only a personally selected part of the truth. Leacock's answer is that the film-maker covers those points which seem to him interesting and important in order to convey reality. He is objective in the sense that he does not create what he films-- he discovers it. He claims that "it's no less objective to be selective."[41] Like other exponents of this style, he denies any pretensions of presenting a great, overall truth.

> Obviously we have our own bias and selection, obviously we're not presenting the Whole Truth. I'm not being pretentious and ridiculous: we're presenting the film-maker's perception of an aspect of what happened ... what it was like to be there when it happened. You make up your own mind....[42]

Leacock does not use a hidden camera for capturing reality, as was sometimes Vertov's approach. He does not believe in spying on people, but admits that by using this technique, a lot of useful footage can be obtained which otherwise would be impossible to come by.

The immoral thing to him is to portray something false and pretend it is real. He believes that film-makers should "find out some important aspect of our society by watching our society, by watching how things really happen as opposed to the social image that people hold about the way things are supposed to happen. "[43] When the film-maker reveals such discrepancies he is holding a mirror up to people in which they can learn something important about themselves, because as a result of modern communication, especially film and television, people have invented a whole new set of clichés.

> We think we know things, but actually these are distorted or completely wrong or have the vital thought taken out of them. I have a deep feeling, for example, that I know what happens in a law court.... And my so-called deep feeling about what happens in a law court actually comes from movies that I've seen that in turn were very likely made by people who had never been in a law court either. And what we are getting is the formation of self-perpetuated cultural myths, which can get more and more inaccurate. [44]

Leacock also cites Hollywood's treatment of war, and specifically World War II, as another example of how Hollywood creates misconceptions. They make war fast and dramatic and organized rather than the slow, wearying, strange, and terrible thing that it is, which is so hard to define or portray. As noted in Chapter IV, the neo-realism movement in Italy, after the war, demanded more realistic presentation of war subjects because experience denied the Hollywood myth, and thereby it foretold the advent of a cinema closer to true life experience.

It is Leacock's opinion that such realistic presentation in cinema, as against the fictional method, is essential to the proper education of a society--education not in the formal schoolroom sense, but in the more significant sense of people getting to know themselves and their society.

> ... How is a national point of view changed? I don't think most white Americans have the faintest idea what discrimination is, what it's like to be born black and to be condemned to a role in life because of this accident of birth from the day one is born. People think that discrimination is being refused admittance to a restroom. But that's only one end of it. It's far more subtle and profound than this. Now, I haven't the foggiest idea how you do it in terms of this kind of filming, but I believe it is possible. [45]

Leacock believes that filming incidents in the lives of blacks is far more effective than writing about or lecturing on problems involved in racial discrimination. He says,

> You have to see it to believe it. This kind of filming has to be done by Negroes. It can't be done by whites. When I intrude into a private Negro home in the South, I just know that all the conversation changes. The distortion is enormous. All of a sudden you get 'front-parlor-white-talk.' And all the human, all the marvelous things just cease. [46]

Leacock admits that there is no large audience yet for his kind of film and so they have no place on television, which tries to reach a vast number of people--although it was television that first sponsored these attempts, at least in America. The film industry also has little interest in using short films, particularly of this kind. But he believes that cinéma vérité film-makers must learn to be satisfied with smaller audiences and greater power of communication-- more or less exchanging communicative quantity for quality. Repeated screenings have proven that many people are eager to see such films, but the problem is to organize and attract the audience which is known to exist. [47]

Leacock does not believe in mixing fiction or controlled filming with reality, but he admits that his approach can have application in controlled filming. "Jean Renoir is one who is very aware of this, for instance--the actors in his films become a sort of poem; the whole huge technical machine, and the director, stand in the background, without intruding." [48]

To Leacock, then, there are two kinds of films--the theatrical and the real. Theatrical films stem from fiction and go in the direction of theater. Leacock thoroughly approves of and enjoys this type of film unless it pretends to show reality while applying a theatrical grammar, in which case he believes it will ultimately not work because one can see all the unreal elements in it. The "willing suspension of disbelief" is for admitted fiction, not for so-called "reality." The other kind of films, such as he among others is making, comprises those which truly have to do with reality. [49]

These films have nothing to do with the artifice of theater or drama; they stem from the drama in real life.

They are authentic. And that, to Leacock, is the most important quality of a film. Like Zavattini, the Italian neorealist, Leacock believes that people in real situations create drama, and that the film-maker must record it within the established discipline of this style, i. e. , by discovery rather than intrusion.

Leacock, like Rouch, admits that he is dealing with a very narrow band of the spectrum of film-making, but he believes that if it is further explored and applied to other kinds of film-making, it will revolutionize the whole film industry.

NOTES

[1]Ulrich Gregor, "Leacock oder Das Kino der Physiker--Ulrich Gregor im Gespräech mit dem amerikanischen Filmaker Richard Leacock," Film, 4, Jahrgang, Heft 1 (Januar, 1966), p. 14.

[2]Ibid.

[3]Ibid.

[4]Ibid.

[5]Ibid, p. 15.

[6]Gideon Bachmann, "The Frontiers of Realist Cinema: The Work of Ricky Leacock" (from an interview conducted by Gideon Bachman), Film Culture, Nos. 22-23 (Summer, 1961), pp. 13-14.

[7]Ian Cameron and Mark Shivas, "Interviews," Movie, No. 8 (April, 1963), p. 16 (interview with Richard Leacock).

[8]Bernard Dort, "A Cinema of Description," Artsept, No. 2 (April-June, 1963), p. 129.

[9]André S. Labarthe et Louis Marcorelles, "Entretien avec Robert Drew et Richard Leacock," Cahiers du Cinéma, Vol. XXIV, No. 140 (Fevrier, 1963), p. 25.

[10]A. William Bleum, Documentary in American Television (New York: Hastings House, 1965), p. 125.

[11]Louis Marcorelles, "The Leacock Experiment," Cahiers du Cinéma, Vol. XXIV, No. 140 (Fevrier, 1963), pp. 15-16.

[12]Luc de Heusch, The Cinema and Social Science: A Survey of Ethnographic and Sociological Films, No. 16, 1962, p. 57.

[13]James Blue, "Thoughts on Cinéma Vérité and a Discussion with the Maysles Brothers," Film Comment, Vol. II, No. 4 (Fall, 1965), p. 27.

[14]Gregor, op. cit., p. 16.

[15]Bachmann, op. cit., pp. 16-17.

[16]Bleum, op. cit., p. 198.

[17]Claude Julien, "A Man in the Crowd," Artsept, No. 2 (April-June, 1963), pp. 45-48.

[18]Bleum, op. cit., p. 194.

[19]Blue, op. cit., p. 22.

[20]Blue, op. cit., p. 23.

[21]Blue, op. cit., p. 27.

[22]16mm, B and W, 72 minutes. Camera: Auricon. Recorders: Nagra and Stellavox. Synchronization system: Accutron. Photographed by Richard Leacock, Donn Alan Pennebaker. Directed by Gregory Shuker. Produced by Robert Drew.

[23]Armando Plebe, "Il 'Cinema-Verità: Ragioni e Pericoli di Una Moda," Filmcritica, Vol. XIV, No. 137 (Settembre, 1963), p. 516.

[24]Cameron and Shivas, op. cit., p. 18.

[25]Bleum, op. cit., p. 195.

[26]Louis Marcorelles, "Nothing but the Truth," Sight and Sound, Vol. 32, No. 3 (Summer, 1963), p. 115.

[27]Cameron and Shivas, op. cit., pp. 16-17.

[28]Ibid., p. 17.

[29]Jonas Mekas, "Notes on the New American Cinema," Film Culture, No. 24 (Spring, 1962), p. 9.

[30]Ibid.

[31]Cameron and Shivas, op. cit., p. 18.

[32]16mm, B and W. Camera: Auricon. Recorder: Nagra. Synchronization system: Accutron. Photographed by Richard Leacock, Donn Alan Pennebaker. Produced by Drew Associates.

[33]James Blue, "One Man's Truth, an Interview with Richard Leacock," Film Comment, III, No. 2 (Spring, 1965), p. 19.

[34]Patricia Jaffe, "Editing Cinema Verite," Film Comment, Vol. 3, No. 3 (Summer, 1965), p. 46.

[35]Blue, "One Man's Truth," p. 17.

[36]Ibid., p. 20.

[37]Jaffe, loc. cit.

[38]Labarthe et Marcorelles, op. cit., p. 19.

[39]Bachmann, op. cit., p. 14.

[40]Ibid.

[41]Blue, "One Man's Truth," op. cit., p. 16.

[42]Cameron and Shivas, op. cit., p. 18.

[43]Blue, "One Man's Truth," op. cit., p. 18.

[44]Ibid.

[45]Ibid., p. 19.

[46]Ibid.

[47]Ibid.

[48]Bachmann, op. cit., p. 23.

[49]Blue, "One Man's Truth," op. cit., p. 21.

CHAPTER X

DIFFERENCES IN APPROACH

The approach to cinéma vérité film-making by Europeans--in particular the French film-makers--differs fundamentally from that of the American group. James Blue aptly puts it,

> The Europeans are eclectic, unitarian. All ways lead to the Truth-God. They intervene, probe, interview, provoke situations that might suddenly reveal something. There is an attempt to obtain from the subject a kind of creative participation. The Americans are, for the most part, fundamentalists. They eschew all intervention whatever its goal. They cultivate an alert passivity. They seek self-effacement. They want the subject to forget that they are there. [1]

Typical of this generalization are Jean Rouch in France and Richard Leacock in the United States. In this chapter an attempt will be made to clarify some of the principal differences between the methods of these two cinéma vérité pioneers, which represent the general approach followed in this kind of film-making in Europe and the United States.

Rouch and Leacock have always shared a belief that people in real situations will produce a drama worthy of capturing for cinema, much more valid and interesting than any fabricated version of it. But beyond this point the two film-makers differ greatly in their approach. To Rouch, cinema is an instrument of communication between the director and his actors, among the actors themselves, and between the audience and the screen. He stresses the importance of rapport between the film-maker and the subjects being photographed. Without this rapport, he believes the truth cannot be brought out. As an example he cites the Drew/Leacock film, Nehru. He points out that the film did not work because of a lack of contact between the subject and the filmmaker, until a particular question was put to the Prime Minister.

Rouch uses the camera to "plumb the depths of the conscious." He considers it a catalyst which somehow encourages people to talk freely about what they really think and feel. The camera makes them aware of themselves by giving them a feeling of importance and a new insight into their lives, providing an emotional outlet. Therefore, Rouch considers what goes on in front of the camera to be less important than the fact that the camera is there.

To Leacock on the other hand, the camera is only a tool. What is important to him is to capture the reality discovered by the film-maker in front of the camera. This reality is more than just the facts--it includes the emotions, the atmosphere, the very essence of life. He neither prepares nor provokes that reality or creates situations. He wants to become integrated into a given milieu, to capture without interfering those sparkling moments of truth which sometimes reveal themselves. [2] Certainly no actor can produce such remarkable feeling of truth as is created in The Chair when the lawyer hears of his client's pardon over the phone and bursts into tears. Drew (while working with Leacock) once commented that they liked to be present at the time "when man comes against moments of tension and pressure, revelation and decision. "[3]

For Leacock no contact with the people that he photographs is necessary. He wants to photograph them in such a manner that the presence of the camera and the film-maker in no way interferes. He wants his subjects to be so involved in what they are doing that they forget the presence of the camera and the film-maker. This is why he states that the only thing that happens to people in Rouch's films is that they are being photographed.

As can be seen, the camera serves a different function for each man. For Rouch it is a stimulant, a catalyst, a mirror, a device that opens windows in the lives of his subjects. But for Leacock the camera has only one function--that of recording. Leacock in this respect follows Vertov's theory of photographing people without their being aware of the presence of the camera and the film-maker.

Rouch's ideal for cinéma vérité is to build fiction with reality, using non-actors and improvised techniques. In some of his films he used a fictional or improvised situation to plumb the depths of an underlying reality. Leacock's approach in "Living Camera" is to "catch life unawares," while Rouch chooses people who have a story to tell. As one analyst has said, "Rouch incites his subjects to talk in order to provoke encounters and discussions that induce them to 'play' involuntarily or voluntarily in a given role. He, himself, once said, 'What fascinates me in this kind of cinema is to see how easily human beings create something new--another person altogether for good or ill....'"[4] He places non-actors in a suppositional situation and lets their conversation reveal their true feelings on the designated subject. Leacock comments, "I believe that Rouch is going in the direction of the theatrical, staged films and that we're going in the opposite direction."[5]

To Leacock, mixing of fiction and reality is not acceptable. He believes that if fiction is introduced, one must use real actors and thus produce conventional cinema in the direction of theater. For purposes of cinéma vérité, or as he calls it, "Living Camera," he is not interested in improvisation from a given situation, nor in discussing one's self through a form of cinematic group therapy. He wants to show a real situation, both factual and emotional, letting the truth of the situation reveal itself in the natural course of events. The viewer is thus allowed to form his own opinion, find his own answers, as if he were watching the actual happening. He rejects Rouch's approach when he says, "... the films of Rouch give carefully thought-out answers to problems ... we if anything attempt to give evidence about which you can make up your own mind."[6] And Rouch states, "What amazes me about Leacock is that I have found him with a mind closed to all other films.... I regard Leacock as a reporter. He is consumed by information, which I find horribly mechanical."[7]

What seems to be surfacing from these comments by the two film-makers representing the European and the American style is the cultural differences which affect the philosophy of style of each man. To the puritanical-minded Americans, "truth, and nothing but the truth" is of utmost importance, and once the truth has revealed itself, the conclusion is generally left to the viewer. But perhaps to the French, carefully thought-out conclusions are more effective, more penetrating than "nothing but the truth."

Paul-Louis Thirard, a French writer, criticizes the work of the Drew-Leacock team from a slightly different viewpoint: "The case of the Drew-Leacock team poses better than any other the problem of deception in cinéma vérité ... because ... they are the most serious, the most honest, the least sharp and even the most naive."[8] Continuing his evaluation of their work he points out, "Less than ever does the objectivity of the camera permit the person responsible for the film to 'wash his hands of it'; more than ever, the fallacy consists in making the honestness coincide with an impossible non-involvement."[9]

A. William Bleum, an American cinema critic, says, "The issue, at bottom, is that if we are told we are seeing actuality then any tampering with human action and emotion within a scene will to the degree that it is committed, weaken the entire idea of documentary."[10] As has been discussed, Leacock, unlike Rouch, was adamant in refusing to "tamper" with action and emotion.

In short, Rouch and Leacock both want to find the reality of life through their individual cinematic approaches which are highly influenced by their different cultural backgrounds. They seek to uncover the truth in people that is hidden under the superficiality of their daily lives. Rouch wants to pierce the surface truth to reach underlying reality by means of discussion, interview, and improvisation. Leacock wants to capture the same underlying reality by photographing people, without intruding. He believes this can be achieved when the subject is too involved or too tired to hide what he really feels and is. As one analyst comments, Rouch seeks to unmask truth through a process of deliberate self-revelation, while Leacock seeks to convey truth through capturing unguarded moments of self-revelation in the movement of real life. In other words, Rouch wants to explain the raison d'être of life, whereas Leacock wants to let it reveal itself.

Once photography of the events is concluded, the approach of the two men in editing also differs widely. Leacock believes in editing his material to a coherent form, faithful to the chronology of the event. He says, "We don't just shoot it and show it. We edit it, to get across the feeling we want."[11] He often finds new and exciting drama in the material that was not apparent while covering the event. But to Rouch, ideally, editing has no place in cinéma vérité film-making. He likes to show what he photo-

graphs untouched. For this reason, and because of the im-
practicality of showing lengthy films such as the original
21-hour version of Chronique d'un Eté, he has learned to
choose subjects which are strictly limited in time, and then
to shoot only the essentials of an event.

The extreme differences in approach and philosophy
culminated in bitter confrontation when Rouch and Leacock
met in debate at the Lyon cinéma vérité conference. Louis
Marcorelles points out,

> ... in fact the evident hostility between their points
> of view suggested not merely an incompatibility be-
> tween two different ways of looking at things, but
> even in a sense between two rival forms of civiliza-
> tion, the French and the Anglo-Saxon. Leacock
> postulates a kind of cinematic Rousseauism, with
> echoes of his master, Flaherty: let us uncover
> people and objects in their natural state, rediscover
> the motion of reality, and we will return the cine-
> ma to its primary function, that of revealing the
> beauty of the world. For Rouch, whose admiration
> for Flaherty is no less extreme, the thing is to
> avoid the too easy truths, to try always to pene-
> trate to the source of that social comedy which
> primitive and civilized life alike impose on us. [12]

Other critics, also, have pointed out that Leacock's
films do not reveal the universal man, but the American man.
Jean-Claude Bringuier writes: "America is really the author
of Leacock's films. "[13] He adds, "He is devoted to ...
people who bustle about completely absorbed in what they are
doing, and whose very private life is almost made public. "[14]
On the other hand, it may be said that Rouch's films reveal
only the Frenchman. The truth revealed by any cinéma
vérité film emerges from, and applies to, only a given culture rather than necessarily having a universal application.

Leacock claims that Rouch prevents people from being
themselves when he forces meanings from them according to
a pattern he has arbitrarily set, while Rouch criticizes Leacock for being too uncritical and accepting whatever comes
along as part of "the American way of life. " The argument
remains unsolved, but perhaps Rouch's method is most appropriate to the French love of logic and need to refine in-
tuitions to an equation expressed in love of the spoken word,
while Leacock's approach is best suited to an action-oriented

nation, to surging American life built on a hero-champion concept, with its restless, ceaseless movement in an unending drive for success. Each man represents the philosophy of an approach in cinéma vérité film-making followed and exercised on two different continents.

NOTES

[1]James Blue, "Thoughts on Cinéma Vérité and a Discussion with the Maysles Brothers," Film Comment, Vol. II, No. 4 (Fall, 1965), p. 23.

[2]Louis Marcorelles, "L'Expérience Leacock," Cahiers du Cinéma, Vol. XXIV, No. 140 (Fevrier, 1963), p. 13.

[3]Gideon Bachmann, "The Frontiers of Realist Cinema: The Work of Ricky Leacock" (from an interview by Gideon Bachmann), Film Culture, Nos. 22-23 (Summer, 1961), p. 18.

[4]Eric Rohmer et Louis Marcorelles, "Entretien avec Jean Rouch," Cahiers du Cinéma, Vol. XXIV, No. 144 (Juin, 1963), p. 4.

[5]Ulrich Gregor, "Leacock oder Das Kino der Physiker --Ulrich Gregor im Gespräech mit dem amerikanischen Filmaker Richard Leacock," Film, 4 Jahrgang, Heft 1 (Januar, 1966), p. 19.

[6]Ian Cameron and Mark Shivas, "Interview," Movie, No. 8 (April, 1963), p. 18 (interview with Richard Leacock).

[7]Rohmer et Marcorelles, op. cit., p. 8.

[8]Paul-Louis Thirard, "Drew, Leacock and Company," Artsept, No. 2 (April-June, 1963), p. 44.

[9]Ibid.

[10]A. William Bleum, Documentary in American Television (New York: Hastings House, 1965, p. 204.

[11]Bachmann, op. cit., p. 23.

[12]Louis Marcorelles, "Nothing but the Truth," Sight and Sound, Vol. XXXII, No. 3 (Summer, 1963), p. 115.

[13]Jean-Claude Bringuier, "Libres Propos sur le Cinéma Vérité," Cahiers du Cinéma, Tome XXV, No. 145 (Juillet, 1963), p. 16.

[14]Ibid.

PART IV:

VARIATIONS ON A THEME

CHAPTER XI

OTHER PIONEERS AND PRACTITIONERS

1. Mario Ruspoli

In France cinéma vérité is as closely associated with
Mario Ruspoli (b. 1925) as with Jean Rouch. A former
painter and journalist, Ruspoli, like many other French directors of the nouvelle vague period, came to the film medium with no prior training in conventional cinema. He rejects Jean Rouch's term cinéma vérité and--like those in
The American School--prefers to call his style "direct cinema." He maintains:

> The combination of the words 'cinema' and
> 'truth' is meaningless. The camera may be pres-
> ent and hidden, it may be psychoanalytical or inter-
> rogative, but it does not thereby come closer to
> seeing the 'truth,' nor does it know any more about
> it than we ourselves see and know. [1]

Ruspoli says that the human eye or the camera eye can only
record bits and pieces of truth because it is impossible to
encompass all aspects of truth simultaneously. [2]

He points out that even Dziga Vertov was not trying
to capture "truth" when he spoke of cinema truth (Kino-
Pravda); rather, he sought authentically to portray events for
the purpose of informing or teaching. Cinema truth is an
accurate means of informing, not of capturing "truth" and
never an end of "truth" in itself. To achieve this, "... the
film maker ... is called upon to display the utmost sincerity,
the maximum degree of self-effacement vis-à-vis the events
which he films but must never induce." [3]

Ruspoli's contribution to cinéma vérité, or as he prefers to call it, direct cinema, is more in the line of sociological documentary than the interviews and fictional stories

toward which Rouch leans. "Where Ruspoli probes what already exists, Rouch likes to create his situations and subjects at the actual moment of filming."[4] Ruspoli is more interested in the Vertovian type of film, "a non-interventional research cinema documenting social life, events, the behavior of the individual, the group and society."[5] He is mainly concerned with recording on film only what is real, spontaneous and true, rejecting at the same time what he calls three typical documentary film attitudes: "the 'picturesque' and 'paternalistic' attitude"--the tourist-trap film; "the 'propaganda' documentary attitude"--a film slanted to support preconceived ideas of what should be done about a given situation; "the television-journalism attitude"--the quick interview aimed at the spectacular, which too often distorts and reverses the truth supposedly presented.[6]

Although differing in some areas of approach, Ruspoli and Rouch exhibit certain similarities, according to Raymond Borde:

> ... Rouch and Ruspoli want to grasp inimitable
> existence at this inimitable moment where it is
> only itself. In old-fashioned 19th Century language,
> we could say that they want to photograph the Life
> Force Mosaic. They report the rising gesture,
> and words which jostle each other. They bribe the
> subjective faces of the world, hoping to plumb the
> soul's depths and in this sense there is something
> of the cop in them![7]

Ruspoli defines three criteria to distinguish direct cinema from other types of film-making; they are worth noting:

1. Sight and sound in synch. and on the spot, using light, silent and portable equipment, seeing as little as possible, and allowing the film maker to shoot spontaneously under any kind of conditions....

2. A new way of working. Directors and technicians must know how to work 'like one man.' They are often in the position of forgetting or seeming to reject most of the classical cinema principles, so as to devote themselves to these new means of expression and discovery.

3. The film maker's attitude of observation and
    research consists in drawing substance from
    the same elements in life, of society, of man-
    kind, and of duty without transforming them,
    just as they appear to our eyes or our camera.

    This last criterion is especially important. It
    allows a distinction between the vérité directors
    and some of their predecessors. [8]

Among Ruspoli's many films three are of particular
importance to direct cinema style: Les Hommes de la
Baleine (1956), a study in whaling in the Azores Islands,
photographed by himself; Les Inconnus de la Terre (1961), a
survey of the living conditions of a section of the rural population in Lozère; and Regard sur la Folie (1961), a film on
aspects of life in a psychiatric hospital, Saint Alban, Lozère.
Ruspoli himself particularly classified the latter two films
(made with Michel Brault as cameraman) as good examples
of direct cinema.

In his Preface to Les Inconnus de la Terre ("The Unknown of the Earth")[9] Roland Barthes says that Ruspoli, with
the help of Michel Brault and Jean Ravel, "was able to make
an equitable film which clarifies and seduces at the same
time" and adds,

    But yet, despite the temptation of the subject
    that equitable film is not an obscure film: a
    savour, a warmth, a cleanness move about through
    the pictures; the objects, the words, a reciprocal
    reliance puts a live vibration between the camera
    and these men, these landscapes, between the
    questioners and the questioned. [10]

This movie grapples with the problems of isolation,
under-population, and the difficulty of achieving adequate production. Regard sur la Folie ("A Look at Madness")[11] endeavors to communicate the "feeling of madness"; it shows
the various activities of patients' groups in occupational
therapy, psychotherapy, and sociotherapy, ending with the
hospital's annual celebration.

Ruspoli generally aligns himself with the American
school of cinéma vérité, rather than with Jean Rouch, of
whom he writes, "... he carves out of life his own ideas.
Therefore he 'shows' people. He does not 'get in'...."[12]

Nevertheless he includes Rouch's Chronique d'un Eté in his list of the best films which in varying degrees fit his definition of direct cinema. [13] Unlike Rouch, however, but like Leacock, he believes that the cinema team should be self-effacing, blending into the background in such a way that it has the least possible effect on the subject.

He gives specific advice on how this can be accomplished, suggesting that the cinematographer carry his camera equipment as unobtrusively as possible, know how to conceal himself in a crowd, avoiding abrupt gestures and speaking as little as possible (particularly to his team-mates), and how to be quietly friendly to the people about him. In short, he must "merge with the background." He should behave in such a way that the reaction is, "that's certainly not the cameraman."[14]

Ruspoli writes about a rather amusing experience he and his team-mates, Pierre Lhomme, Etienne Becker and Antoine Bonfanti, had while shooting Petite Ville (1962). [15] They spent their first day linked together by the synchronization wire as they ran in and out, through the dense crowd of the 14th of July parade. On the following day, Ruspoli was astonished to see three members of his team participating in the traditional sack race organized for children--filming and recording as they hopped along beside the little contestants in the race. To his amazement, the pictures were very sharp and hardly at all "shaky."

He believes that Leacock's team of two persons is unrealistic in light of the heavy technical demands on such a team; he prefers four men--sound engineer, cameraman, cameraman's assistant, and director, perhaps adding the editor as a fifth. * Although he ranks the sound engineer's job as most important, these men must all operate as equals; they must not only be outstanding technicians but also psychologists (innate or trained), physically able, and of superior intelligence and sensitivity. They--especially the editor--must be of exceptional moral integrity so that they will avoid in any way using or abusing the truth they are recording. Because the cinema team should make every effort not to intrude upon or into the situation, the editor should cut

---

*It should be noted here that Mr. Ruspoli's statement was made in the 1960s when camera and sound recording equipment had not been improved, as it is today.

the material only "to give the facts, to analyze and to inform the public, to make it conscious of the human and social problems which need to be solved. "[16]

Ruspoli foresees a promising future for direct cinema:

> It is obvious that direct-cinema constitutes a new and fundamental element in the dissemination of culture at all levels. It represents an enormous advance in capturing reality, and even doing so in a sense of continuity. Thanks to its simplicity and the economy of its structure, it can revivify the television of the present and future. Its applications are universal and purely and simply replace all those of the traditional cinema, including the fictional field. The doors of the studio no less than the doors of men's homes lie open to it. [17]

2. Jacques Rozier

Jacques Rozier (b. 1926), a French film-maker who has used cinéma vérité methods for fictional stories, gained most of his experience in television, working on short films. He made Rentrée de Classes in 1955 and Blue Jeans in 1958 before he embarked on his first feature, Adieu Philippine (made in 1961, released in 1963). The film is about one hour forty-five minutes long and was produced by Carlo Ponti. Adieu Philippine is a fiction film to which Rozier applies methods of cinéma vérité, closely following Jean Rouch's style, and is considered to be an excellent example of such applications.

Rozier believes that three things constitute the important factors in the making of films: music, situation and dialogue. He further believes that sound is more important than image in determining the editing. He says, "I think that rhythm which first strikes the spectator is in the sound rather than in the picture. The ear is more sensitive than the eye. "[18] In editing Blue Jeans he arranged cuts to coincide with the music--cutting on strong beats and loud notes.

Both Rouch and Leacock had hoped to apply their methods of photography to fiction films, but it was Rozier who actually did so. Rozier is of the opinion that the future of fictional films in cinéma vérité style lies in the direction of using lightweight equipment, improvisation technique, and other "free" cinematic methods.

At Lyon, where the French radio-television organization sponsored a conference on cinéma vérité in 1963, some critics objected to the presentation of Adieu Philippine at the conference as a representative of cinéma vérité films. However, it is the opinion of many critics, including Roy Armes, that "its chief qualities are its youthful vitality and the improvised, Cinéma-Vérité style, authenticity of the language, characters and settings."[19] Cameron and Shivas, who interviewed Rozier in Paris after the Lyon conference, call it:

> ... the Nouvelle Vague's finest achievement to date.
> It brings many of the methods of Cinéma-Vérité to
> the fiction film.... With the appearance of truth
> that these methods can produce, Rozier gives Adieu
> Philippine a peculiar poignancy and lyricism by his
> use of setting, his use of montage and music.[20]

Rozier wrote a script for this film which is a combination of two scripts--one, the story of a young French boy who goes to Algeria for his military service, showing him before being drafted as a gay and carefree youth and after completion of service entirely changed (a script he thought would be rejected by the French censorship); the other, a musical comedy on two 17-year-old girls who are great friends until they meet a boy who goes out first with one and then the other, thus making the two girls enemies. Adieu Philippine is built around a television cable boy in France who is called off to military service at the time of the Algerian war. Before joining the service he meets two girls who are great friends and takes them both out alternately in Paris, spends his holiday with them in Corsica, and has an affair with each of them before going off to Algeria, thus making the two girlfriends great enemies.

His lead in the film is a bank clerk, selected out of 500 candidates, none of whom had had any previous acting experience. He was chosen, according to Rozier, only because of the way he spoke "titi Parisian." Rozier told his actors generally what he wanted and let them improvise as they went along. He dubbed the film after completion, using an exact transcription of the original dialogue to guide his actors in producing the precise intonations required. Because of his method of improvisation, he photographed more than 130,000 feet for one hour and forty-five minutes of completed film. Another factor contributing to this very high ratio of shooting was that he often used three cameras simultaneously, a method deriving from his television experience. Rozier believes: "Film for a director is just like paper for a writer. "[21]

Adieu Philippine cost seven million (old) francs, including distribution and publicity, and took one year in the making including five months for dubbing and editing.

Although Adieu Philippine is a fictional story, photographed in the tradition of the feature film, it is a hybrid in that Rozier utilizes cinéma vérité methods and techniques to achieve his ends. Many critics believe that Rozier's approach in cinéma vérité is a combination of the styles of other exponents--that he has plucked a flower from each garden. Mark Shivas expresses this idea well when he says,

> ... like Rouch he sets a pattern for his characters
> to follow, but here it is entirely fictional. Like
> Leacock's camera, Rozier's seems to be accepted
> unself-consciously and to be neither controlling the ac-
> tion or making a comment on the characters. The
> natural performances and settings, and Rozier's use
> of music to stress the symbolic and lyrical pas-
> sages, produce a feeling of reality stronger than
> many of the murky, awkwardly-focused reportages
> shown at Lyon. His improvisation produces a
> result as 'true' as anything springing from directly
> recorded life. [22]

Rozier believes that the future of cinéma vérité lies in the direction of applying these techniques to fictional stories.

3. Chris Marker

Chris Marker (b. 1921) is considered the one true essayist of the French cinema. He has a wide range of interests and employs diversified styles in film-making. He began his career as a writer and journalist, and came to cinema like so many other young film-makers of nouvelle vague in the early 1950s, without any previous film experi-

ence. He made his first 16mm documentary film on the
Finnish Olympic games in 1952. Marker has made films
ranging from animated cartoons (Les Astronautes, 1959, in
collaboration with the Polish cartoonist Walerian Borowczyk)
to conventional documentary (Description d'un Combat, 1960)
to fictional films in kinestasis style (Le Jetée, 1962, made
entirely with still photographs). Each of his films shows the
imprint of his personality and reveals his unique personal
approach.

One of Marker's early efforts was the film Lettre de
Sibérie (1957), made while on a trip to the Soviet Union.
For him, Siberia is a land of contrast "situated between the
Middle Ages and the 21st century, between the earth and the
moon, between humiliation and happiness. "[23]

The film is made up of a variety of different materials:
newsreel shots, travelogue footage, still photographs, and
even animated cartoons. Marker shot the film mostly in
color, but introduced some excerpts in black and white and
some in sepia. Roy Armes says,

> ... Talking of mammoths and cave dwellers, he
> shows a picture of a prehistoric artist at work--
> none other than Bernard Buffet. When dealing with
> the reindeer he pauses to give a television com-
> mercial presented by 'United Productions of Siberia'
> in praise of this animal, concluding 'Accept no im-
> itations, always ask for: Reindeer. '[24]

Armes adds, "It is Marker's own sincere but irrev-
erent enthusiasm for the subject that holds the film together
and makes it a satisfying whole. "[25]

Marker's contributions to cinéma vérité are Cuba, Si
(1961) and Le Joli Mai (1963). [26] The latter is the less personal of the two and, therefore, might more properly be
classified as a film in the cinéma vérité style. Raymond
Bellour says, "it is the loveliest cinéma vérité film done up
to now...."[27] The film is a study of Paris in May of 1962,
the first month of real peace for France since 1939. It follows very much the principal idea used by Jean Rouch in his
Chronique d'un Eté, with the exception that Marker's focus is
on a broad social and political spectrum while Rouch deals
with a limited group. Marker uses the interview technique
to examine the private lives and happiness of a wide range
of people in Paris and tackles controversial issues such as

the Salan trial and the problem of Algerians living in France.
The film is three hours long, shot in 16mm and enlarged to
35mm for theatrical showing.

Some critics believe that Le Joli Mai achieved the dimension of a masterpiece of sociological investigation into
the various problems that Parisians had to face on the eve
of the Algerian war. Unique in its field and bearing the imprint of its makers' personalities, it is at once a statement,
a lyric, an analysis, and an indictment. Unfortunately, it
was not possible to show it commercially in its full-length
version, and the film-makers were compelled to shorten it
to a two-hour version. Viewers who have seen both versions
believe that what was removed is as rich and interesting as
the rest of the film.

Peter Graham, one of the severest critics of cinéma
vérité, says about Marker's style:

> Chris Marker's more personal approach is dif-
> ferent from that of Drew-Leacock or the Maysles.
> In films such as Cuba, Si and Le Joli Mai, he ex-
> amines his own conscience in a poetical rather than
> analytical way. This kind of method is full of haz-
> ards, as the films of Herman and Reichenbach
> show by their faults. But Marker's sensibility and
> control are such that he never once puts a foot
> wrong. [28]

Then Graham compares Marker's Le Joli Mai with
Rouch's Chronique d'un Eté and concludes that Marker's
achievement is a work of art:

> ... [His interviews] are combined with more lyrical
> linking passages where Marker evokes his own vi-
> sion of the city. For him, the expressive re-
> sources of the cinema are not anathema. Shots
> and sequences are not strung sloppily one after
> another in misguided imitation of reality, but form
> part of an organic whole.... The music also plays
> an important and subtle part.... Whereas with
> Rouch the commentary is virtually abjured, with
> Marker it constitutes the binding element; subdued
> but full of sinew, it guides the spectator persua-
> sively through the film and up to its moving con-
> clusion. [29]

Le Joli Mai, structured mainly around interview technique, is also considered by some critics to be one of the fine contributions of France to cinéma vérité. Unlike his other films, Marker uses his personal commentary only to open and close Le Joli Mai. The people's comments on themselves and their personal problems are much more interesting than their comments on the big issues of the day, which were originally supposed to serve as the uniting element in the film.

Writing about Marker's films, Roy Armes says that they are "at one and the same time adult meditations on existence and nostalgic evocations of a childhood world coloured by Jules Verne and American Superman comics."[30]

His approach may often appear whimsical, frivolous or satirical, but he deals seriously with the struggle of men to free themselves from the past and to build a better society.

Raymond Bellour has said that Marker, "being in love with Film, conveys his joy better, perhaps, than anyone else."[31]

Chris Marker's concept of cinéma vérité is well represented in his famous statement, "Vérité n'est pas le but, mais peut-être la route" (vérité is not the end, but perhaps it is the way).

4. Albert Maysles

As discussed in previous chapters, cinéma vérité in the United States developed and flourished with a number of journalists and film-makers gathered together under the leadership of Robert Drew in Drew Associates. James Lipscomb, Drew's assistant, recalls:

> ... we didn't have any theories about cinéma vérité when we started. We actually started as journalists out of Life magazine trying to capture on film some sense of reality which we didn't see in most of the television programs of the time; and of course, we didn't see in theatrical films. [32]

Among the most notable of the group were Robert Drew,

Richard Leacock, Donn Alan Pennebaker, James Lipscomb, Gregory Shuker, Hope Ryden, and the Maysles brothers. Because of the importance of Showman, a famous cinéma vérité film produced by the Maysles brothers, they have been singled out from among the rest for particular mention.

Albert Maysles, once a psychology teacher at Boston University, collaborated with the Drew Associates until 1961 and, together with Leacock, Pennebaker and Shuker, photographed the early classics of the American cinéma vérité films--notably the famous Primary. After leaving the Drew Associates, Albert and his brother David (who records the sound and does the editing) formed a team and made a number of films in cinéma vérité style: Showman (1962), What Is Happening? The Beatles in the U.S.A. (1964), Meet Marlon Brando (1965), Salesman (1969), Gimme Shelter (1970), and others. The most important and controversial of their films is Showman, [33] a 53-minute film on Joseph E. Levine. The film is a study of the famous American film promoter during the period when he was handling the Loren/de Sica picture Two Women, [34] a story of the vicissitudes that accompany the conclusion of a big film and publicity deal.

The brothers followed Levine from New York to Cannes, where he met Sophia Loren (star of Two Women) at the Cannes Festival, and on to Boston, Hollywood and Rome, filming some of his activities in private and public situations and hoping for a big business deal to break as a climax to their film. Altogether they spent about three weeks with Levine but, unfortunately, nothing of significance happened and they had to be content with filming his day-to-day activities. Luckily, during a reunion with one of his old friends, Levine revealed something about his childhood poverty; also during this period Sophia Loren won an Academy Award for her performance in Two Women. These two events saved the Maysles film from being a mere recording of Levine's diurnal activities. Some critics believe that the film, in essence, attempts to examine the world of the American big businessman, intelligently and sincerely, by photographing authentic situations as they unfold. It is not surprising, therefore, that some 30,000 feet of film were shot during these three weeks, out of which less than 2,000 feet were used--a ratio of approximately 15 to 1.

Because Levine would not give his approval, the film was not released to the general public in the United States, but it was entered in many film festivals in Europe and re-

Top: Joe Levine making a deal in his hotel room in Cannes. Below: Levine and Sophia Loren in her apartment in Rome when he gave her the Oscar for the film, "Two Women" (both from SHOWMAN). Photos courtesy of Maysles Films, Inc.

ceived much acclaim from some European critics. James Blue reports that the film "... provoked both earsplitting protest and thunderous praise. "[35] When it was shown in Hollywood, "... the prestigious members of the lofty Motion Picture Academy saw ten minutes of 'SHOWMAN' and stopped the projection!"[36]

Showman was also presented at the Lyon cinéma véri-te conference. Some of the controversial remarks of the critics concerning this film are worthy of mention:

> Among the many European critics who praise the film, Peter Graham in Films and Filming said that 'the film showed, I think, the tremendous possibilities of reportage technique. In contrast to Jean Rouch, the Maysles are more concerned with using their technical skill (which is greater than Rouch's) to record reality without tampering with or imposing on it. '[37]

The French critic, Louis Marcorelles, who calls Albert Maysles the most brilliant of contemporary cameramen, says of Showman:

> ... the most disregarded, the least well understood of all the films at Lyon, seemed to me to be the most beautiful, the most pure. I would readily classify it with some ten or fifteen great films that I have had occasion to see since the war. I affirm this view for after three successive viewings, at Lyon, at Paris, and in London, far from a dwindling enthusiasm, I think on the contrary it has grown. [38]

In Hollywood, the film was considered by many to be too critical of the "industry," and in New York, a "whitewash" of both the industry and Levine himself.

James Blue says, "Old school documentarists call it 'anti-audience' and 'anti-art. '"[39]

Louis Marcorelles reports,

> 'We just like to make movies, ' was Al Maysles' rather splendid answer to an aggressive Roberto Rossellini ... who criticized the Maysles for not producing 'art' and for sacrificing too much to a

Above, David Maysles (sound) and
Albert Maysles (camera) filming
Paul Brennan in SALESMAN; opposite, Salesman Paul Brennan pushing the Bible (photo by Bob Adel-
man).   All photos courtesy of
Maysles Films, Inc.

dangerous modern passion for the formless and shapeless. [40]

Marcorelles goes on to say that the Maysles brothers were able to show the truth about the man (in action) in Showman--albeit a truth that was not altogether pleasing:

> In a mad world, Joseph Levine, the most lucidly mad of them all, rules over all without effort. He is the sore in the living flesh of the American society, the symbol of a social mechanism which has become delirious, but each second on the screen he remains a man, our brother, with all his dimensions, and in each of his sentences, intonations, like the nostalgia of a somewhere else, of a lost paradise where life would really have a meaning. [41]

Another Maysles brothers' film, Salesman (1969), [42] is a full-length production, a penetrating study of four door-to-door Bible salesmen, Jimmie, Ray, Charlie, and Paul Brennan. The film follows the salesmen as they try to push mostly disinterested or perplexed customers into buying a $49.95 Bible which the majority of them cannot afford, even on installments. The four salesmen have been assured in a sales conference that theirs is a holy mission, which appeals to the American moral man, but they, particularly Brennan (who is portrayed in the film at greatest length), are discouraged by the lack of response they encounter. The film is humorous in the sense of true comedy which is rooted in tragedy. The emptiness of the lives of the salesmen and their customers is contrasted with beliefs represented by the book they are selling.

Another one of their films entitled Gimme Shelter, also photographed in 1969 (with Charlotte Zwerin as co-director), covers certain events in a tour of the Rolling Stones (a rock music group) across the United States. This film is particularly dramatic because the tour ends in outright mayhem.

It was on a Saturday in early December of 1969 when the Rolling Stones gave the final performance of their American tour (an open-air affair) at a speedway track in Altamont, California, 15 miles east of Berkeley. Patrick MacFadden writes,

> The Hell's Angels were retained to preserve

law and order.... This they did with enormous
expertise and inverted lead-tipped billiard cues,
gunning their glittering motorbikes through the yaw-
ping groupies like tigers loose in a chicken
coop....[43]

This was the setting for the tragic drama that ensued:

> One unfortunate who had removed all his clothes
> in a fit of solidarity with Nature was savagely put
> upon by the Angels, short on sympathy for such
> middle-class displays. Finally one 18-year-old
> black, Meredith Hunter, bearing a gun and pursuing
> some lonely odyssey inside his own head, fell under
> the knives of the Angels, and was hacked to death.[44]

Accustomed to disorder and hysteria in their audiences,
the Rolling Stones continued their concert, pathetically unaware that the "fracas" up front was not a run-of-the-mill
"rumble" between gangs or an ordinary free-for-all fight.
But their manager saw it all and, foreseeing real trouble,
whirled the Stones away in a helicopter, "leaving disaster
below."[45]

MacFadden's appraisal of the film follows:

> 'Gimme Shelter' is a technical knockout, a
> blindingly well-realized experience of the tensile
> furies that leap along the filament of human greed
> and aesthetic expression.[46]

The philosophy of the Maysles brothers, like that of
Richard Leacock, is that there must be no directing, no intervention on the part of the film-maker in cinéma vérité
style. Albert Maysles further rejects the interview technique
as a device in cinéma vérité films and believes that the film-
maker must always remain a mere observer. It is for this
reason that his approach is considered to be the "purest" in
the American cinéma vérité school. Maysles believes that
everything comes out of nature, out of life, and that a film-
maker should go directly to these sources for his material.
He is mainly interested in revealing the inner character of a
subject, rather than treating it with a journalistic approach.
Working with an Auricon camera and an Angenieux zoom lens
especially modified by the two brothers, Albert Maysles uses
the camera as an observer and believes that only one camera
should be used in filming because the viewer becomes the

Top: Mick Jagger performing at Madison Square Garden. Below; Jagger, with the Maysles brothers, sees the stabbing at Altamont on the Steenbeck editing machine. Photos from GIMME SHELTER, courtesy of Maysles Films, Inc.

one camera; the camera eye becomes the spectator's eye.
He photographs in one continuous shot and does not believe
in reaction shots.   He feels that most documentary films with
no synchronous sound are merely surface realism.   "What
kind of realism can you achieve in a movie when you can't
even hear anybody talking?"[47]   He calls such films "illustrated lectures."

Contrary to Flaherty, who studied his subjects thoroughly before filming, Al Maysles is of the opinion that

> The better you know somebody, the more you
> are at a disadvantage.   You are no longer curious
> to put down things familiar to you.   The essential
> you let go by, because you say to yourself: 'Every-
> body knows that.'[48]

Furthermore, he believes that when the film-maker
meets people for the first time they reveal more of themselves than later on in the relationship.   He admits, however,
that the personality of the film-maker has a lot to do with
how artful a cinéma vérité film will be.   He states:

> ... even though in this style of Vérité one is de-
> pendent 100% on what is before the camera--what's
> happening by itself--one is also dependent 100% on
> who is filming it.   And it can come out hot or cold.
> Those people who are not putting art into Vérité
> films ... something is holding them back from
> being like Cartier-Bresson.[49]

Albert Maysles says that our obligation is to be honest
with what we film, and James Blue expands on this thought:

> Because of Al's avowed purpose to catch a kind
> of 'subjective-objective' truth, his cinema is one in
> which ethics and aesthetics are interdependent,
> where beauty starts with honesty, where a cut or a
> change in camera angle can become not only a pos-
> sible aesthetic error but also a 'sin' against Truth.
> In things cinematic, Al Maysles is a religious
> zealot.[50]

5. William C. Jersey, Jr.

The son of very religious parents who thought that

there was something evil about cinema, William Jersey
(b. 1928) came to be a successful film-maker in cinéma vérité style. His most important contributions are Search into
Darkness, Prisoner at Large, Manhattan Battleground, Incident on Wilson Street; and perhaps his best films are A Time
for Burning and Goodbye and Good Luck.

Jersey started his film career as an art director with
a small film company near Philadelphia. In 1954 he studied
documentary film-making at the University of Southern California and two years later went to Peru as a sound recordist
to work on a feature film for Warner Brothers, working with
producer Tom McGowen. After this, he worked with Willard
Van Dyke and Graham Ferguson on a film in Alaska in which,
under the supervision of Van Dyke, he did some of the photography. In 1961 he made a film for Willard Van Dyke
called Search into Darkness, which incorporated all the elements of a cinéma vérité film. His first attempt at photographing cinéma vérité style was to shoot the film with a
35mm BNC camera mounted on a crab dolly. He says, "I
use that as a reference to why I feel cinéma vérité--as far
as I am concerned--is more of an attitude, than equipment. "[51]

If, as James Blue states, "Cinéma-Vérité has its or-
thodoxies, its heresies, its unitarians and its fundamentalists, "[52] William Jersey is a combination of all of these. In
his films he seeks to catch the dramatic elements of real
life--people at moments of crisis--and to make social comment; in this search, he utilizes the most desirable techniques of each cinéma vérité practitioner to achieve his goal.

As discussed in previous chapters, many cinéma vérité pioneers rely exclusively on "found" events. Jersey is
not content solely with the truth he can capture by waiting or
by chance. He says,

> I discovered that by understanding the people
> and their needs I could make suggestions which
> would benefit both them and the film. They were
> freed to react honestly because they were not acting
> for the film but for themselves. [53]

He believes that the film-maker somewhat alters reality by his mere presence, so why not guide the elements in
his favor? He comments: "I would like the films to be
more a function of art and less a function of accident. "[54]
Then he points out that a cameraman is seldom on the spot

when something significant or dramatic happens in life; it is
wiser for him, therefore, to act as catalyst, to bring together the potentials of a situation so that he can be there
when the important moment comes. Properly handled, this
guidance does not change the truth or integrity of the subject.
He says,

> I do not limit myself to those situations that by
> accident or another's design will occur in my pres-
> ence when I am ready and able to film. I see no
> reason why I should not explore; for instance, if I
> am interested in the work of a social worker, as in
> MANHATTAN BATTLEGROUND, I ask him whom
> might he see that day and then encourage him to
> see those individuals whom I think he would inter-
> act with in ways that would reveal him and his en-
> vironment in a meaningful and organizable way. [55]

Pursuing this philosophy, he brought together the minister and the Negro barber in A Time for Burning (1966)[56]
and recorded their conversation as they confronted one another for the first time. This film is the true story of the
step-by-step ordeal of the Augustana Lutheran Church in
Omaha, Nebraska, when a modest plan for improving race
relations, through integration with nearby Negro churches,
meets stiff resistance from white parishioners. The film
chronicles the controversy that ensued among church leaders,
along with the resultant resignation of the pastor, and gives
startling insight into the honest feelings of those involved.

Jersey has said that by understanding people and their
needs, he can make suggestions and then they are free to
react. He gives one excellent example from his experiences
in filming A Time for Burning:

> ... I suggested to a white minister of an affluent
> all-white church that he see a particular Negro
> barber who could effectively articulate the frustra-
> tion and anger within most Negroes.... The min-
> ister cared enough to hear this viewpoint but had
> not sought out this man. I was not concerned that
> the minister might not have ever gone to see Ernie.
> I was very concerned about what the sweat on his
> brow told me about the Rev. Youngdahl, and what
> the biting phrase, 'Your Jesus is contaminated,'
> (expressed without surface feeling) told me about
> Ernie Chambers. [57]

Two shots from A TIME FOR BURNING, produced by Quest Productions for Lutheran Film Associates. Above, a Lutheran pastor hears from a bitter Black barber in Omaha. Below, church leaders react to a modest plan for improving race relations.

Jersey always selects a subject that he cares about because he believes that then there can be an audience that also cares about it. He tries to find people who externalize-- show what they are, what they feel and think--and a catalytic situation which will reveal who they are.

He structures his films during the editing process. In A Time for Burning, for example, a three-hour conversation among five people in the film was edited into a four-minute segment. In this way he believes that he captures the "Truth," the heart of what the characters are saying, rather than "truths"--a faithful, chronological reproduction of actual, repetitive, hesitant conversation. In essence, he is more interested in communicating emotions than facts, the drama behind the obvious external appearance of situations and people.

A Time for Burning was shot by Jersey alone, but he claims that ideally a cinéma vérité film should be made with two cameras, one to photograph the action and one the reaction, because "film making is more reaction than it is action."[58] His film Incident on Wilson Street basically portrays the reaction of a child, her parents, her teacher and her fellow students to the fact that she struck another child. One does not see the striking action, only everyone's reaction to the event that has happened.

William Jersey summarizes his approach to cinéma vérité as follows:

> In the reality I observe around me I see no heroes--just ordinary humans who can, on occasion, exhibit rather extraordinary, even heroic behavior. For those who wish to see or portray the world as it is with all its complexities, ambiguities, its terror and delights, what has happened to Cinéma Vérité is good.... It has provided a frame of reference against which the superficial or artificial can be measured, and fictional (as well as other documentary) films will continue to be affected by this new standard![59]

The very crux of his philosophy lies in this statement: "We may find fewer heroes in films, but we may also find more insight into real people, and therefore into ourselves. That's worth something."[60]

6. Other American Practitioners

As was noted, the purpose of this chapter is to discuss a number of French and American cinéma vérité pioneers whose works were of particular significance in the development of this style of film-making. There are other film-makers, however, both in Europe and the United States, who have contributed greatly to the early development of this movement and deserve a place in this chapter, but who can not be mentioned because of the limitations of space.

Because of the importance of a number of American film-makers who applied some of the principal approaches of this style to the feature film industry in the United States, and for the first time broke away from the conventional way of film-making in Hollywood, a few have been selected for discussion here. These film-makers, who became strongly influenced by the emergence of cinéma vérité, produced a number of films using this approach, albeit not totally within the grammar of the style. One may call them indeed the nouvelle vague group of the American commercial cinema.

Swayed by the historical development of various styles that brought about the cinéma vérité movement, and encouraged by courageous rebellions in the arts and crafts of cinema in Europe, these film-makers in America revolted against Hollywood and its conventional approach to film-making. They started making their films with unknown actors and actresses, on extremely low budgets (sometimes as low as $15,000--unheard of at the time), on location rather than studio sets, and with basic production equipment and minimum means at their disposal.

Under these hardships their reward was to have complete control over their films. Thus they left a distinct imprint of their own personalities on the films they produced, and thereby initiated in the United States the kind of film commonly referred to as "cinema of the author."

To make their cinematic efforts commercially successful, and in order to break through the conventional system of distribution, some even established their own theaters. A prime example is Lionel Rogosin, who opened the Bleecker Street Cinema to show his Come Back, Africa after he had been turned down by many distributors and theater owners. Rogosin is one of the directors who distinguished themselves in producing such films on the periphery of the cinéma véri te style. Two of his most significant films are On the Bowery (1956) and Come Back, Africa (1958).

In the former film Rogosin introduces the viewer to a group of derelicts who live in a world of their own in the well-known district of New York City called the Bowery, where they have formed little groups to combat loneliness. Most of the despairing population of the Bowery is made up of alcoholics, prostitutes, mental defectives, unemployables and some who have just given up and are waiting to die. When Rogosin decided to portray the life of these people he found it necessary to choose a few individuals as representatives of the whole heterogeneous group.

Luc de Heusch says, "It was decided that the actors, chosen on the spot, should express themselves freely, in their own slang, should carry out familiar actions without restraint, but in accordance with a preestablished dramatic line based on actual cases.... The important scenes called for the positive co-operation of the 'actors' and allowance had to be made for their unstable natures, not to mention trouble with the police. "[61] He goes on to say, "This astonishing document is without precedent in cinema history. "[62]

Rogosin made Come Back, Africa under the pretext of making a report on the mines in South Africa, when in reality his purpose was to make a film depicting the wretched conditions under which the black workers were forced to live. The resulting full-length feature film is a sensitive portrait of the inequities suffered by a people under a system ruled by apartheid.

Rogosin says about his approach, "to make reality enthralling and significant is an artistic process. The people to be described must be allowed to live freely, but an effort must be made to fit them in with the themes which the producer discovers in their behavior. "[63] He believes that a great amount of preparation is necessary to carry out such a plan, as was true in making both of his films, On the Bowery and Come Back, Africa. In the first one Rogosin plotted his approach by studying all aspects of the situation in order to satisfy himself that he would arrive at the truth as he saw it. In Come Back, Africa Rogosin invited the collaboration of two Africans in putting together his "scenario, " to ensure a reasonably accurate interpretation of the facts.

His motives, like those of other cinéma vérité practitioners are noble, as reflected in his statement, "I want to give a man a new dignity ... to make a true national hero of a Nebraska farmer, a Pennsylvania coalminer, a Harlem taxi driver. "[64]

Another American director who distinguished himself in this kind of film-making is John Cassavetes, who produced Shadows in 1958. The film has no real plot and was shot without a script. It is in fact made up of improvisations on the everyday life of a Negro family, two brothers and a sister. The viewer senses the interrelationships of members of the family (experiencing with them the tender moments as well as the quarrels), and at the same time feels the mood of the city in which they live. Most of the film was shot at night, and so presents, in the main, night people in bars and on dark, forbidden, lonely streets.

The younger generation received the film with exuberant enthusiasm, because--in their thinking--Cassavetes succeeded in "telling it as it is." However, commercial distributors found it shocking and persuaded Cassavetes to re-shoot and re-edit the film. Unfortunately, the second version loses some of the spontaneity and freshness of the original, similar to what was experienced by Rouch in his Chronique d'un Eté.

The film was shot on 16mm at a cost of only $15,000 and later blown up to 35mm, proving that a great outlay of money, as used to be common practice in the Hollywood film industry, is not necessary for the production of an exciting, worthwhile film.

Film Culture, in its editorial "A Call for a New Generation of Film Makers, " wrote: "Shadows proves that a feature film can be made with only $15,000. And a film that doesn't betray life or cinema. What does it prove? It proves that we can make our films NOW and by OURSELVES. Hollywood and the miniature Hollywoods of our 'independents' will never make OUR films. "[65]

Jonas Mekas compares Shadows with the works of Truffaut, Jean-Luc Godard and Jean Rouch in Moi, un Noir, and says, "What 'Shadows' (first version) did was to use, often to perfection, many elements which are among the essential characteristics of the New American Cinema and which, very often, correspond to the characteristics of the Nouvelle Vague film makers. "[66]

Robert Frank and Alfred Leslie particularly distinguished themselves through a tragi-comedy entitled Pull My Daisy (made in 1959) which has most of the characteristics of a cinéma vérité film. The film is a free improvisation on a theme involving an ex-drug addict, Milo (a railway worker) and his wife. The wife, wishing to pull her husband up to a respectable middle-class style of living, through religion, enlists the cooperation of a young self-ordained "Bishop."

An evening of conversation and music, beer drinking and poetry reciting in Milo's home, with the Bishop and his family and some of Milo's poet friends as guests, provides the fabric out of which the film is made. The Bishop's mother plays the organ while his sister blows the bellows. "They talk, drink beer, discuss God, play trumpet, talk again. Nothing much happens.... The camera harshly and pitilessly reveals the bedroom, the sink, the table, the cockroaches. "[67]

The film-makers have said, "The conflict of identities is inevitable and here it is sharpened. Exactly ... who is who ... what is what ... why is why ... how is how. It is a mad evening, an insane visit, a heroic and bedraggled circle. "[68]

Jonas Mekas says, "No other film has ever said so much, in such a pure and condensed manner, about the man of the beat generation," and adds, "Its authenticity is so effective, its style so perfect, that the film has fooled even some very intelligent critics: they speak about it as if it were a slice-of-life film, a piece cut out from the raw stream of life, a documentary. "[69]

An interesting but totally non-cinéma vérité approach in this film is its sound track. The film was photographed silent and Jack Kerouac later added the commentary as well as speaking the parts of the characters. Kerouac was asked to provide the lines for each character without previous study of the film--a treatment similar to that given by Jean Rouch to Moi, un Noir. Mekas says that Kerouac's commentary "has immediacy, poetry and magic that is without precedent in American cinema. "[70]

These and other young American film-makers, highly influenced by the emergence of new and free styles of film-making in Europe and the United States during this era, courageously produced a number of feature films that followed the basic approaches of cinéma vérité style and thus gave birth to what is known as the New American Cinema.

NOTES

[1]Mario Ruspoli, "Towards a New Film Technique in the Developing Countries. The Light-Weight Synchronized Cinematographic Unit" (UNESCO Report to Second Beirut Round-Table on "Arab Cinema and Culture," October 28-30, 1963, W. S. /1063.1 CUA). Paris, 1964, translated from the French and mimeographed, pp. 14-15.

[2]Ibid., p. 14.

[3]Ibid., p. 15.

[4]Roy Armes, The Personal Style, French Cinema since 1946 (Amsterdam: Drukkerijen vh., Ellerman Harms NV, 1966), Vol. II, p. 126.

[5]Ruspoli, op. cit., pp. 15-16.

[6]Ibid., page 15.

[7]Raymond Borde, "Problems of Cinéma Vérité," Monthly Cinema Review, No. 49, Paris, December, 1962 (translated by Charles H. Sweeting), p. 6.

[8]Raymond Bellour et Jean-Louis Leutrat, "Préface," Artsept No. 2, Le Cinéma et la Vérité (Avril/Juin, 1963), p. 6.

[9]16mm, B and W, medium length. Camera: Coutant-Mathod KMT. Recorders: Nagra Neo-Pilot and Perfectone. Synchronization system: Pilot-guided. Photographed by Michel Brault, Roger Morillère. Sound: Roger Morillère, Danielle Tessier. Assistant: Dolores Grassian. Editors: Jean Ravel, Mario Ruspoli. Directed by Mario Ruspoli. Won "Prix de la Critique" at the Tours International Short Film Festival.

[10]Roland Barthes, Preface to "Les Inconnus de la Terre," Artsept, No. 2 (April-June, 1963), p. 76.

[11]16mm, B and W, medium length. Cameras:

Coutant-Mathod KMT. Arriflex. Recorder: Nagra. Synchronization system: Pilot-guided. Photographed by Michel Brault, Roger Morillère, Mario Ruspoli. Sound: D. Tessier, D. Grassian, R. Morillère. Editors: Henri Colpi, Henri Lanoe, Jacqueline Meppiel. Directed by Mario Ruspoli.

[12]Mario Ruspoli, Letter to the author, March 26, 1967.

[13]Ruspoli, "Towards a New Film Technique ..." op. cit., p. 36.

[14]Ibid., p. 26.

[15]Ibid., p. 25.

[16]Ibid., p. 30.

[17]Ibid., p. 30.

[18]Ian A. Cameron and Mark Shivas, "Interviews," Movie, No. 8 (April, 1963), p. 25, (Interview with Jacques Rozier).

[19]Armes, op. cit., p. 135.

[20]Cameron and Shivas, op. cit., p. 23.

[21]Ibid., p. 24.

[22]Ian Cameron and Mark Shivas, "Cinéma-Vérité," Movie, No. 8 (April, 1963), p. 15 ("New Approach," M. S.).

[23]Armes, op. cit., p. 101.

[24]Ibid.

[25]Ibid.

[26]16mm, B and W, full length. Camera: Coutant-Mathod KMT, Arriflex. Recorder: Perfectone, Nagra. Synchronization system: Pilot-guided. Photographed by Pierre Lhomme, Denis Clairvol. Assistant: Etienne Becker. Sound: Antoine Bonfanti. Editor: Eva Zora. Director: Chris Marker.

[27]Raymond Bellour, "Les Signes et la Métamorphose," Artsept, No. 2, Le Cinéma et la Vérité (Avril/Juin, 1963), pp. 132-133.

[28]Peter Graham, "Cinéma-Vérité in France" (Three Views on Cinéma-Vérité), Film Quarterly, Vol. XVII, No. 4 (Summer, 1964), p. 35.

[29]Ibid. , pp. 35-36.

[30]Armes, op. cit. , p. 106.

[31]Bellour, op. cit. , p. 133.

[32]Perry Miller, Interview with Willard Van Dyke, James C. Lipscomb, and William C. Jersey, Jr. , May 16, 1967, New York Film Council (mimeographed).

[33]16mm, B and W, 53 minutes. Camera: Auricon. Recorder: Nagra Neo-Pilot. Synchronization system: Accutron. Photographed by Albert Maysles. Sound and editing: David Maysles.

[34]"Levine is best known for his promotion of Hercules, which he bought for £50, 000, spending £400, 000 on promotion; as a result one out of every eight Americans went to see the film and Levine cleaned up." Cameron and Shivas, "Interviews, " op. cit. , p. 19 (interview with Albert and David Maysles).

[35]James Blue, "Thoughts on Cinéma Vérité and a Discussion with the Maysles Brothers, " Film Comment, Vol. II No. 4 (Fall, 1965), p. 24.

[36]Ibid. , p. 23.

[37]Maxine Haleff, "The Maysles Brothers and 'Direct Cinema, '" Film Comment, Vol. II, No. 2 (1964), p. 20.

[38]Louis Marcorelles, "La Foire aux Vérités, " Cahiers du Cinéma, Vol. XXIV, No. 140 (Fevrier, 1963), pp. 28-29.

[39]Blue, op. cit. , p. 23.

[40]Louis Marcorelles, "Nothing but the Truth, " Sight and Sound, Vol. 32, No. 3 (Summer, 1963), p. 117.

[41]Marcorelles, "La Foire aux Vérités, " op. cit. , p. 29.

[42]A Maysles Films, Inc. , Production, about 90 minutes. Director: David Maysles. Photographer: Albert May-

sles.   Editors: David Maysles and Charlotte Swerin.

[43]Patrick MacFadden, "Gimme Shelter," Film Society Review, Vol. 6, No. 3 (1970), p. 39.

[44]Ibid.

[45]Ibid.

[46]Ibid.

[47]Haleff, op. cit., p. 22.

[48]Blue, op. cit., p. 24.

[49]Ibid., p. 25.

[50]Ibid., p. 24.

[51]Carson and McBride, Interview with William C. Jersey, Jr., March 30, 1967 (mimeographed).

[52]Blue, op. cit., p. 22.

[53]William C. Jersey, Jr., "Some Observations on Cinéma Vérité," Motive, Vol. XXVII, No. 2 (November, 1966), p. 12.

[54]Carson and McBride, op. cit.

[55]William C. Jersey, Jr., "Some Thoughts on Film Technique," Film Comment, Vol. II, No. 1 (Winter, 1964), p. 15.

[56]16mm, B and W, 58 minutes.   Camera: Eclair NPR. Recorder: Nagra. Photographed by William C. Jersey, Jr. Produced by Lutheran Film Associates.

[57]Jersey, "Some Observations on Cinéma Vérité," loc. cit.

[58]Carson and McBride, op. cit.

[59]Jersey, Jr., "Some Observations on Cinéma Vérité," loc. cit.

[60]Ibid.

[61]Luc de Heusch, The Cinema and Social Science: A Survey of Ethnographic and Sociological Films, No. 16, UNESCO (1962), pp. 55-56.

[62]Ibid., p. 56.

[63]Ibid.

[64]Ibid.

[65]Jonas Mekas, "Cinema of the New Generation, Part Two: The New American Cinema," Film Culture, No. 21 (Summer, 1960), p. 10.

[66]Ibid., p. 11.

[67]Ibid., p. 13.

[68]Ibid., pp. 13-14.

[69]Jonas Mekas, "Notes on the New American Cinema," Film Culture, No. 24 (Spring, 1962), p. 10.

[70]Mekas, "Cinema of the New Generation," op. cit., p. 13.

PART V:

TECHNOLOGICAL DEVELOPMENTS INSTRUMENTAL
IN
BRINGING ABOUT CINEMA VERITE

CHAPTER XII

EQUIPMENT

Strangely enough, film as the seventh art has always been at the mercy of its technology. Since its inception the dream of film-makers has been to have equipment with which the physical process of film-making could be made simple. Their goal has been not only simplicity of operation but freedom to be able to dictate their wishes to those monstrous machines rather than have the machines dictate what they could and could not do. The tools of film-making, however, have become more complicated as cinema has progressed: cameras became heavier; cranes, dollies, tracking rails, complicated lighting equipment were added, and with the advent of synchronous sound, cameras were placed in blimps,[1] with the result that enormous sound-recording machines became an integral part of filming. As Mario Ruspoli aptly put it, this "heavy artillery" of film-making has restricted the artistry of the film-maker by requiring an "army of technicians" to handle it.[2] In the old Hollywood days, sometimes as many as 50 technicians were required to work on a normal set. We have come a long way since then, and the technology in cinema has been advancing rapidly.

But the film-maker's most important tool, the camera, is not yet as easy to handle as the painter's brush, the sculptor's clay and chisel, or the writer's pen. The camera for a long time has been a behemoth to whose demands the artist has been forced to submit. Most of the cameraman's efforts, instead of being concentrated on artistic creativity, have been spent struggling with this huge piece of equipment, wondering all through filming whether the camera would do what he wanted it to do; often he has had to give in to the equipment because in this art form it is the machine that sets the limits, not the artist. Jean Renoir, in an interview with André Bazin in 1958, made an

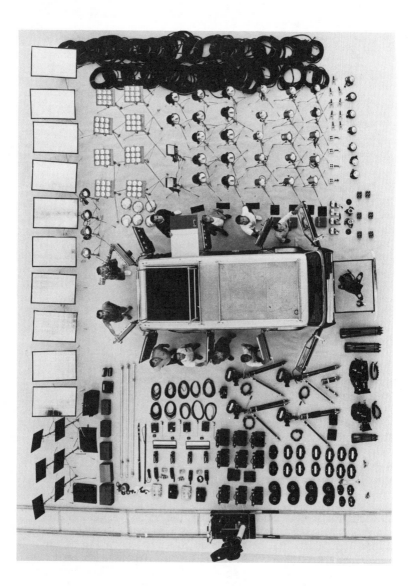

amusing statement which pointed out the problem realistically:

> ... in the cinema at present the camera has be-
> come a sort of God. You have a camera, fixed on
> its tripod or crane, which is just like a heathen
> altar; about it are the high priests--the director,
> cameraman, assistants--who bring victims before
> the camera, like burnt offerings, and cast them
> into the flames. And the camera is there, im-
> mobile--or almost so--and when it does move it
> follows patterns ordained by the high priests, not
> by the victims. [3]

Granted that the massive, cumbersome artillery of the
film art and its army of technicians allowed great technical
resourcefulness which produced fine technical results, but
they also curtailed the creative process of the film-maker.
All through the history of cinema there has been evident a
struggle between the film artist and the tools of his trade--
a struggle for the artist to free himself from the impedimenta of film-making. It wasn't until the mid-fifties that
several important breakthroughs occurred in the technology.

With the advent of television in the late forties, the
16mm film and equipment (introduced in 1923 by Eastman
Kodak Company to place motion picture photography econom-
ically within the reach of amateurs and scientists) acquired
professional status overnight. Laboratories all over the
world, wherever television studios were introduced, were
obliged to set up 16mm facilities to cope with this constantly
growing need. Documentary film-makers grabbed this format as their ideal and economic rescuer. New 16mm equipment and films were introduced into the market to take care
of this ever-increasing professional demand. Nevertheless,
the 16mm equipment was almost as heavy, cumbersome and
bulky as its 35mm predecessors. And the main problem was
still that of achieving easily synchronized sound, particularly
on location.

Although in many cases the 16mm format proved eco-
nomically sound to film-makers working in either television
or documentaries, to those who were after capturing life as

Opposite, a cinemobile, contents and crew. This unit is designed for filming on location in remote areas. [147] Courtesy
of Cinemobile Systems, Inc. of Hollywood.

it is, in its natural background away from the artificiality of the studio sets, the same problems existed. These latter film-makers needed sync-sound equipment small enough not to intrude upon the situation by noise or appearance, and portable enough not to restrict their movements. New 16mm cameras had to be designed to give maximum stability of picture while hand-held, since using a tripod would immobilize the cameraman. Ian Cameron wrote:

> Freedom from tripods may seem a very small gain, but anyone who has made the simplest film will know the amount of time wasted by setting the camera on a tripod. Taking the camera off the tripod is like being cured of a paralysis. No longer is the camera held down to static shots or restricted in its movements. For the maker of a fiction film, the time wasted on setting up shots can be a discouragement. For the makers of documentary and reportage films, it can make things impossible. Events have passed by before the camera can be set up, or showing them would require movements of the camera which could not be managed. [4]

Manufacturers both in America and Europe started to improve the 16mm camera by making the motors and shutters as noiseless as possible, for silencing it with a blimp destroyed its compactness, and therefore its mobility. New ways also had to be found to photograph in synchronized sound while the crew had the maximum capability of free movement.

It was not until 1960 that such 16mm equipment, comparatively light in weight and simple in operation, was sufficiently developed to enable a crew of two people, one working the camera and the other the recorder, to go into any situation and return with material for a film, technically acceptable and with synchronous sound recorded directly at the moment of shooting.

Thus this portable 16mm equipment, which freed the film-makers from creative restrictions imposed by heavy equipment, launched a new style of film-making called cinéma vérité. Patricia Jaffe, a film editor and critic, claims that "The key to the development of direct cinema was a revolution in equipment that allowed for greater flexibility and the use of direct sound. "[5]

In the late fifties, film technicians as well as cameramen started to develop and modify various makes of cameras to meet the requirements of direct photography. The Americans experimented with the 16mm Auricon; the Canadians with the 16mm Arriflex; and the French invented the 16mm Eclair, a camera considered in the 1960s to be the most suitable for this style of film-making.

All three cameras have been further improved in their basic design and ease of operation in the past years, to the point that they are all considered to be equally good, depending on the preference of the cameraman. Others have come into the market such as CP16, GSMO, and recently, EMP by Richter Cine Equipment, Inc., which the manufacturers claim is the smallest and lightest professional motion picture camera in the world.

The American cinéma vérité pioneers generally have preferred the 16mm Auricon, which they especially modified and developed for their purposes. The Drew Associates group, in their first breakthrough, photographed Primary with a 16mm modified Auricon with a zoom lens, using a Nagra recorder running off a separate power supply, and synchronized by means of a Bulova Accutron electronic watch. This concept, as mentioned in Chapter IX, was first thought of by Leacock in an attempt to do synchronous filming without a connecting cable. Ruspoli relates:

> Since no light-weight camera was available in the United States, any more than elsewhere in the world, and since such cameras would be too expensive to manufacture, the Drew-Leacock units had to have recourse to handicraft techniques. They replaced excessively 'noisy' elements in their cameras with specially designed silent parts, but nonetheless relied on such heavy 'portable' 16mm studio equipment as Auricon, etc. [6]

The Maysles brothers, who joined the Drew Associates in 1960, also used the Auricon with some other modifications. One modification perfected by the two brothers was a white indicator fitted on the movable ring of the zoom lens on the camera. It is visible from a distance and shows the soundman, who holds the microphone, the width of the frame assumed by the picture. Depending on the position of this indicator, the sound-man knows whether or not he is intruding on the frame.

Maxine Haleff, in an article published in 1964, writes that the Maysles' equipment is basically an Auricon movement with a zoom lens especially designed by them to cope with their specific needs, and that they constantly strive to improve it. She says about the camera:

> ... Because of the balance, the cameraman can put his hands into his pockets or can hold the lens with both hands to operate the zoom and to change focus. The cameraman can freely observe his surroundings, because the camera rests on the shoulder below the line of sight. At present, the camera runs for two hours on batteries with an electronic system to make the motor run at 60 cycles. The Nagra tape recorder by another means keeps the same speed, thus insuring perfectly synchronized sound. No connection is needed between tape recorder and camera.... [7]

One of the big drawbacks of the Auricon compared with other 16mm cameras in cinéma vérité filming was its weight; the cameraman must be, as Ruspoli puts it, "a regular Hercules" to carry it around. He adds that in spite of their heavy Auricon cameras, Drew Associates, whose most important and unique contribution to direct cinema is synchronization without connecting wires (an important advance in synchronized shooting in the 1960s), managed "through sheer ingenuity and patience, to efface themselves, to get to the heart of events, to shoot at the critical moment and to achieve sequences which seem almost miraculous--'Primary' (1960), 'Eddie Sachs' (1962), and 'The Chair' (1962), among others." [8]

The Canadians, and particularly the Film Board of Canada, have also contributed to the development of cinéma vérité films and equipment. Michel Brault's Pour la Suite du Monde (1962) is an excellent example of the results that can be obtained from the modified and improved 16mm Arriflex, achieved mainly by manufacturing soundproofing bags or portable, lightweight blimps to decrease the noisiness of this camera.*

---

*Since 1967, Arriflex has marketed the new 16BL model, a self-blimped camera designed to take 12mm to 120mm Angenieux blimped lens that reduces the camera noise consider-
(cont. on next page)

The Canadians (to overcome the noisiness of their cameras) further experimented and developed the "long focus" technique of sync-sound filming whereby a camera with a telephoto lens is placed at a distance from the subject, who wears a neck microphone. In this way the noise of the camera is not picked up by the microphone and the person being filmed is unaware of when the camera is rolling; thus the effect on him of the camera's presence is reduced.

As stated before, the French film-makers used 16mm Eclair NPR for most of their cinéma vérité filming and since most cameramen preferred this camera for such filming during those years it is appropriate to delve briefly into its history.

The French inventor, André Coutant, a genius of the cinematic technical world, who designed the famous 35mm Cameflex, the Came 300 Reflex, the Cameflex Tele, the underwater Aquaflex and the Cameflex 16/35 combination, foresaw the future demands for 16mm portable cameras, especially for films made for television. In 1958 he designed a 16mm lightweight camera along the lines of the 35mm cameflex, calling the new one KMT. A simple camera weighing only seven pounds, it was not marketed by Eclair Company, to whom Coutant was under contract, because it was considered too "primitive" to compete with the more sophisticated cameras being manufactured outside of France, especially in Germany. So Coutant designed the new 16mm Eclair NPR, sometimes referred to as the "Coutant" camera. It was an improvement, at least in terms of sales, over KMT, and embodied a large number of technical advancements as compared to other models at the times. [9] The prototype version of this camera was first used in 1961 by Michel Brault in shooting Chronique d'un Eté for Rouch and Morin. Swallow, in Factual Television (1966), discussing the development of 16mm equipment, remarks:

> The problems of camera-weight and camera-noise have been largely resolved by new developments in the production of light-weight cameras, notably the camera designed in France by M. Cou-

---

ably, and has improved the camera further during the past year. The 16 BL, with a 400-foot magazine loaded with film, is claimed to produce only a 31-decibel noise level at a 3-foot distance.

tant and now marketed by the Eclair Company; this
is sufficiently silent for the recording of speech in
an interior close-up, and sufficiently light for a
cameraman to hold it either by hand or by a simple
harness for the duration of a ten-minute take. [10]

An important feature of the Eclair NPR for a cinéma
vérité film-maker who sought to photograph spontaneous action was the speed with which the cameraman could change
the magazine. Ruspoli states:

> To provide for cases where it is desired to
> avoid a break in synchronization, the Eclair cam-
> era has a special feature which, with a little prac-
> tice, makes it possible to remove the exposed
> magazine and fit a new one without stopping the
> motor. [11]

In addition, the new 16mm Eclair camera was sufficiently
quiet to allow sync-sound shooting close to the subject.

However, the camera was not completely ideal for the
cinéma vérité zealot. Andre Coutant, while displaying his
camera at the Lyon Conference in 1963, produced a pen
from his pocket and said, "The camera is still not as simple
to use as this, but we're working on it. "[12] And indeed the
new Eclair ACL is an improvement over the NPR; so are
other 16mm cameras, a number of which were mentioned
previously. The new 16mm Eclair camera soon became popular with the new cinéma vérité film-makers both in Europe
and the United States.

Complete with a transistorized governor-controlled
sync. motor, an Angénieux 12-120mm zoom lens and 400
feet of film in its magazine, the camera weighs just over 20
pounds. Because of its unique design the major portion of
its weight rests on the shoulder of the cameraman, thus permitting steadier hand-holding for longer periods of time without causing excessive fatigue by its weight. To a cinéma
vérité film-maker who had to spend hours with his subject,
waiting for a particular thing to happen, the camera constantly ready in shooting position, this was a major advantage.

The camera has a true reflex viewing system using a
mirrored shutter. The shutter can be set to any opening
from 50 to 180 degrees. When it is closed, the light is

blocked from the film and the mirrored surface reflects the image onto the ground glass directly above the aperture. When the film has been positively positioned for the next exposure, the true reflex viewing (seeing and focusing through the taking lens) eliminates all possibilities of parallex error inherent in rack-over or separate viewing systems. Viewing is continuous and the image is seen magnified 12 times.

With the Eclair NPR it is possible to pan horizontally faster than with comparable reflex cameras before any chatter or "strobe" effects appear, because the shutter, rotating on a shaft which is below the aperture, cuts across the picture horizontally from side to side. [13] Other motion picture cameras have shutters rotating on a shaft which is to one side of the aperture, so their shutters cut down from top to bottom. The Eclair system is better on horizontal pans; the other system is better on vertical pans. Considering that a cameraman pans horizontally more often than vertically in cinéma vérité filming, this new horizontal wiping shutter of Eclair became a particular advantage.

The standard eyepiece on the Eclair NPR had more versatility than any other viewer at the time. It is fully rotating and capable of a double 360-degree swivel. It can swivel for right- or left-eye viewing, for high or low positions (shooting up or down) and for shooting forwards or backwards. The automatic eyepiece shutter closes immediately when the eye is removed from the viewer, and opens automatically when the eye is pressed against the viewer. This eliminates any danger of fogging the film when the eye is removed from the eyepiece. When the eyepiece is set in any aspect of the normal horizontal position, the cameraman is looking along an optical axis exactly parallel to the lens axis, whether he uses his right or left eye. Thus, when he opens the "other" eye to check the off-screen action, he is looking right where he should be. When the optical axis of the eyepiece is not parallel to that of the lens, the cameraman who opens the "other" eye is looking off across to one side of the screen. The eyepiece has the widest range of adjustments for individual eyesight, permitting more cameramen to use viewers without glasses.

The camera is not self-blimped in the usual connotation but is a basic design utilizing components that were specially engineered to be noiseless. The motor is comparatively silent and the drive from the motor to the shutter is direct without gears. Mario Souto comments:

The outstanding characteristic of this camera
is its careful engineering, which provides in effect,
noiseless running without sacrificing portability by
the use of blimps. This has been achieved by sim-
plifying to the utmost the noise producing components
in the mechanism. These mechanical modifications
have created the camera's particular shape, which
contributes to its convenience for hand-held shooting. [14]

The 400-foot coaxial magazine is designed to be more
compact and eliminates many problems that exist in the dis-
placement type of magazine. In the latter type the very size
of the magazine often creates problems, such as with wind
on exterior locations or with low overhead clearance, and
the shifting of weight from front to the rear can be a problem
in hand-held shooting. Each magazine takes either core loads
or daylight spools of 100-foot, 200-foot, or 400-foot capacity.
The magzine is accessible from both sides and, as soon as
core load film is engaged in the sprocket wheel of the magazine feed chamber, the remainder of the threading operation
may be carried on in daylight. For this reason no threading
is required when changing magazines. The magazines snap
on and off instantly and have noise-making clutches and loop
guards to disengage drive and to warn of malfunction. A
pop-up button for core flange or spool simplifies unloading.

Eclair NPR is usually supplied with a standard two-
position turret, one for camerette CA-1 lens mounts and one
for "C" mounts. The turret is also available with two CA-1
mounts or two "C" mounts. Any lens from 5.7mm focal
length upwards may be used without affecting the sound level
of the camera. The CA-1 is a heavy, precisely constructed,
instant change bayonet mount without springs or other loose-
fitting adjustments.

For cinéma vérité filming, however, the turret was a
great drawback, because whenever the cameraman wanted to
change frame he had to turn the turret and refocus for the
new lens, thus interrupting the continuity of shooting. A
satisfactory solution came with the variable focal length zoom
and optical Pan Cinors developed by various technicians including Berthiot and Richter, which made it possible to vary
the focal length from 16mm to 60mm while filming. The
Angénieux firm then improved upon this principle and finally,
in 1962, came up with the new 12mm to 120mm zoom with
exceptionally good quality and definition.

The historical development of the zoom lens may be of interest to the serious student of cinema. In an interview, with the authors, Kenneth Richter recalled:

> During the first days of World War Two, I heard of an early, good zoom lens made by Busch in Rathenow, Germany. The plant was bombed flat, and only a very few of the 25-80mm f2.8 Busch Vario-Glaukars survived the war. I was able to buy one in Switzerland only because it was out of order. I repaired it and used it for a time. After trying to get Busch's refugee company in Gottingen to make others (they simply couldn't) I loaned mine for six months to SOM Berthiot. They studied it, coated the lenses for me, and came out with a much simpler Pan Cinor 20-60mm which was far from ideal, but which sold like hotcakes, being the only one around. I finally took my Vario-Glaukar to St. Héand, where a man named Pierre Angénieux, who had an 18-man cinder block optical shop in the sheep meadows outside of St. Etienne, was making some waves with a computer-assisted design of a 25mm f0.95 lens for 16mm cameras. I wound up loaning M. Angénieux the Vario-Glaukar which he wanted to study to see if he could make a zoom. He used it as his 'point de départ' for the evolution of his 17-68mm f2.2 which was the first good 16mm zoom.

The zoom lens enabled the cameraman to obtain frames from a 12mm wide-angle to 120mm telephoto with all the intermediate frames, simply by operating a bar. This lens became the ideal and, in fact, the only lens for the cinéma vérité film-maker who in the process of filming must be able to go from one angle to another immediately. When the Eclair camera is used for cinéma vérité, it is fitted with a zoom lens. However, because of its turret capability, other lenses can also be used if so desired.

The film transport mechanism in the NPR is designed to use a single pulldown claw and a single registration pin movement which also permits the use of single-perforation film. The film is advanced by the cam-driven claw and is positioned against the wedge-type registration pin which engages the perforation immediately below the one engaged by the claw. This diminishes and controls the effect of any inaccuracies in film sizes and perforation placement, and as-

Ken Richter with the EMP 16mm, world's smallest professional cine camera, which Richter invented.   Weight, loaded
with 100 ft. of film, is 1. 2 kg.

sures that the film is held steady during exposure. During
exposure and transport the film is positioned and supported
in a long film channel with a spring-loaded side pressure
plate which is part of the camera aperture plate. The back
pressure plate, with its center stage to assure a flat film
plane, is part of the magazine. When the magazine is removed, the complete aperture, aperture plate, film channel,
and side pressure plates are open and accessible for inspec-
tion and cleaning. Because the magazines snap on and off in
seconds, the cameraman can easily check the gate and aperture without causing delays.

The standard motor for the NPR is a silent transistorized governor-controlled motor operating at a constant
speed of 24 frames per second, from 12 to 15 V. D. C. battery power supply. It incorporates a sync-pulse generator
which, when used with a professional 1/4-inch tape recorder
like the Nagra (developed by Stefan Kudelski) or Stellavox
(developed by Georges Quellet), permits perfect synchronization of sound and picture. The motor is self-correcting with
. 2% of speed. There is a pilot light in the motor which
goes off when the speed varies more than . 2%. In practice
the intensity of this light is also an extra check on battery
efficiency.

The motor has a built-in voltage regulator and will
maintain speed as long as the voltage does not drop below
12 V. D. C. In normal operation it draws 2. 0 amperes. The
sync-pulse is a 1. 2 V. A. C. current of 60 cycles per second
(HZ). Camera body, motor, viewfindings, magazines, and
lens are separate units. Any of them can readily be removed
for cleaning, travel, maintenance or repair. [15]

It may be appropriate to state that cinema in general
and cinéma vérité in particular owes its improved sync-sound
capability more than anything else to the Swiss engineer Stefan
Kudelski, the man behind the Nagra tape recorder, who, in
1958, first made it possible to record sync-sound with a
portable lightweight tape recorder using 1/4-inch tape. For
the cinéma vérité film-maker nothing was more encouraging
than to have a tape recorder light enough to carry around
and capable of running in synchronization with the camera.
The fundamental idea of this system is simple. During photography the camera, which has a built-in sync. generator,
supplies a sync. signal that is recorded on the tape simultaneously with the dialogue, thus making it possible to obtain
a new magnetic film in sync. with the picture. Other such

tape recorders, and in particular the Stellavox, soon appeared
on the market; but for the sake of brevity and particularly
because both American and French film-makers have used
Nagra in most of their cinéma vérité films mentioned in this
book, [16] some important features of the Nagra will be discussed here.

The regular Nagra is a small, portable machine
(12-1/2" X 8-3/4" X 4-1/4") weighing only 13 pounds, 13
ounces, although pocket models of this recorder have also
been introduced lately. It uses 1/4-inch tape and has three
speeds: 3-3/4, 7-1/4 and 15 inches per second. It takes
five-inch reels with its lid closed and seven-inch reels with
its lid open. It has Direct and Reproduce (low impedance)
headset monitoring while recording. A two-watt loudspeaker
system is incorporated into the machine for small group lis-
tening, but a separate battery-operated loud-speaker/amplifier
is also available for stage playback (Model D-H). "Line out-
put" is available during recording or playback at 600 ohms,
about +15 dBm. The machine has 38 transistors, 15 diodes
and one zener diode. High frequency bias is used on both
record and neo-pilot sync. heads. The entire system operates at a regulated 10.5 volts. One microphone input is
provided. A low-level line input is for use with an accessory
microphone pre-amp (BS) or connecting cable, when the camera is operating at 24 frames per second. The signals are
recorded on the magnetic tape by means of a "pilaton" or
"neo-pilot" recording head. In the event of slight variations
in the speed of either camera or recorder during the filming
process, variations of the 60 HZ signal are recorded on the
tape, since the frequency will have varied accordingly. These
variations are then adjusted in the studio by a "resolver"
during re-recording to a sprocket-driven magnetic film. [17] This
method of synchronization, widely used in both feature production and documentaries, had one great disadvantage for the
cinéma vérité film-maker--namely, the necessity of the connecting synchronizing wire between camera and tape recorder. It hampered the movement of a cinéma vérité team
following their subject and was often in danger of breaking,
particularly when the camera crew was working in a crowd.
Yet it has been used in shooting such classic cinéma vérité
films as Chronique d'un Eté and Pour la Suite du Monde.
The manufacturers of film-production equipment have now
eliminated this linking wire between the camera and the tape
recorder with the introduction of crystal sync. components
in cameras and tape recorders. An important technological
breakthrough for sync-sound photography!

The second method of synchronization was by "Accu-tron," developed by the Drew-Leacock team and used for the first time in 1960 in <u>Primary</u>. It became widely popular among the American <u>cinéma vérité</u> film-makers. The principle of this method of synchronization is based on the fact that the camera and tape recorder are both battery-driven but must keep a constant speed during operation and must be regulated accordingly. The Drew-Leacock team concentrated on one of many possible solutions, i. e., one deriving from the Accutron electronic watch (Bulova patent), the mechanism of which is used in spacecraft. The watch operates on the principle of diapason, which transforms the direct current supply by a microscopic battery into alternating current. The Accutron and a transistorized regulator provide the camera with a completely stable current of 60 HZ from lightweight batteries, and can drive the camera motor at an absolutely smooth and steady speed or can supply the recorder with a 60 HZ signal. Theoretically, therefore, by separately attaching an Accutron to the camera and another to the recorder, two independent but completely synchronized machines are obtained. This system, the best devised for <u>cinéma vérité</u> film-makers, enabled the cameraman and sound-man to work in complete synchronization without being linked together. It did not hamper their movements and gave them a freer choice of action. It had one small drawback, however: the Accutron is sensitive to atmospheric variations. If one of the two machines happens to be operating in a place warmer or cooler than the other, there will be variations in the synchronized take, difficult to rectify during editing. But since this peculiarity of the Accutron is well-known, the teams using it can easily guard against such variations. The American <u>cinéma vérité</u> pioneers used this method of synchronization on such films as <u>Primary</u>, <u>Eddie Sachs</u>, <u>The Chair</u> and <u>Showman</u>. [18]

With the above methods of synchronization it is also possible to record the sound through the "micro-transmitter" system in which the sound is picked up via a small shortwave transmitter based on the walkie-talkie principle. The microphone is linked to a tiny transmitter, the size of a cigarette packet or smaller, that the subject carries with him. The sound transmitted through this device is picked up by an equally tiny receiver linked to a portable tape recorder which can therefore pick up and record conversations from long-range, sent by one or several transmitters. The cameraman and sound-man wear earphones so as to follow the action. This system has not yet been developed fully enough to warrant any conclusions. One great handicap is still the quality of the sound recorded, which as a result of going through shortwave transmission is often subject to various interferences.

To establish sync. points on the picture and tape, many methods are utilized. In the early days of cinéma vérité, however, the biggest problem was the synchronization of picture and track. Of the two most popular methods used, hitting the microphone while in camera view was preferred to clap sticks. But today, with the automatic clappers built into cameras as standard equipment, the problem is negligible. While there are various modifications of this automatic method, the basic tool is a small light mounted in the camera body that establishes sync. between film and tape by fogging the film at the head of the roll and putting simultaneous signal on the tape via the sync-pulse cable.

In the operation of the standard automatic clapper in the 16mm Eclair NPR, the clapper light goes on automatically for the first 300 milliseconds after the camera is switched on. While this light is on, the sync. pulse signal is not transmitted to the recorder. When the light goes out, the sync-pulse begins transmission. The clapper light completely fogs about four frames and then dies out gradually during the next four. Sync. is established by lining up the beginning of the sync-pulse on the tape with the first frame following the last completely fogged frame.

When NPR with a "Nagra bloop" modified motor is used with a Nagra recorder, the clapper activates the Nagra recorder's oscillator while the light is on. This puts a 1,000-cycle bloop tone on the tape that is audible in playback. Sync. is then established by lining up the last completely fogged frame with the end of the bloop tone. When it is inconvenient to head-clap the scene, the cameraman may operate the clapper/bloop system manually by pressing a button (which must be specially installed for this purpose) on the motor housing. The bloop tone technique is the one preferred by most cinéma vérité film-makers using the Eclair NPR with the Nagra tape recorder. [19]

For a cinéma vérité film-maker the freedom from having to use artificial lights was just as important as the availability of a portable, noiseless camera and tape recorder with adequate provisions for sync-sound photography. Use of lights not only restricts the activity of the film-maker but

gives an aura of artificiality to the event, to the point that
the natural behavior of the people may be seriously affected.
This problem was solved in two ways. The first was the
introduction into the market of fast film stocks. These are
constantly being improved upon but there still remains a
great gap between the sensitivity of the fastest stocks on the
market and the amount of available light in ordinary homes
and buildings. This gap prompted the second solution, the
"intensification process," which Mario Ruspoli claims is the
contribution of the National Film Board of Canada. Through
this method, the reversal or the negative film stock is force-
processed at the time of developing. A film stock with a
sensitivity of less than 100 ASA can be pushed at the labora-
tory to over 1,000 ASA while still achieving an acceptable
image. When shooting Showman, for example, the Maysles
brothers used Plus-X stock, rated at 64 ASA for tungsten,
with available light, and pushed it to 1,000 ASA in the labo-
ratory and achieved very good results. This intensification
process was a tremendous breakthrough for the cinéma vérité film-makers who have to photograph reality spontaneously
under available lighting. With the improvement of the film
stock it became possible to enlarge a 16mm film of top quality to 35mm of a caliber acceptable for theatrical distribution.
Rouch's Chronique d'un Ete, Brault's Pour la Suite du Monde,
Ruspoli's Les Inconnus de la Terre and Marker's Le Joli Mai
were all enlarged to 35mm for this purpose.

All these technical developments, which are being improved upon constantly, have been significant factors in the
appearance of new approaches in film-making and continue to
give the film artist a more direct personal control, characteristic of other art forms. The tools of the film-maker are
not yet as easy to handle as the painter's brush or the
writer's pen, but with the advancement of our modern technology the film artist can and will be liberated from various
burdensome elements of technicality. The cinema can indeed
escape the dilemma of industrialization and enter the arena
of real art.

NOTES

[1]Soundproof boxes or other encasements in which cameras are placed to prevent their noise from reaching microphones during sound recording.

[2]Mario Ruspoli, "Towards a New Film Technique in

the Developing Countries. The Light-Weight Synchronized Cinematographic Unit" (UNESCO Report to Second Beirut Round Table on "Arab Cinema and Culture," October 28-30, 1963, W. S. /1063. 1 CUA). Paris, 1964, translated from the French, mimeographed, p. 3.

[3]André Bazin, "Cinema and Television, Jean Renoir and Roberto Rosselini Interviewed by André Bazin," Sight and Sound, Vol. XXVIII, No. 1 (Winter, 1958/1959), p. 26.

[4]Ian A. Cameron and Mark Shivas, "Cinéma-Vérité," Movie, No. 8 (April, 1963), p. 12, ("New Methods," IAC).

[5]Patricia Jaffe, "Editing Cinéma Vérité," Film Comment, Vol. III, No. 3 (Summer, 1965), p. 43.

[6]Ruspoli, op. cit., p. 11.

[7]Maxine Haleff, "The Maysles Brothers and 'Direct Cinema'," Film Comment, Vol. II, No. 2 (1964), p. 20.

[8]Ruspoli, loc. cit.

[9]Ibid.

[10]Norman Swallow, Factual Television (New York: Hastings House, 1966), p. 199.

[11]Ruspoli, op. cit., p. 22.

[12]Cameron and Shivas, op. cit., p. 13.

[13]This design is used for the focal plane shutters of some of the best still cameras--Nikon, Leica, etc.

[14]H. Mario Raimondo Souto, The Technique of the Motion Picture Camera (edited by Raymond Spottiswoode; New York: Hastings House. Communication Arts Books, 1967), p. 109.

[15]Eclair Corporation of America Manual (Los Angeles: The Corporation, August, 1966).

[16]Nagra was used for Primary, Eddie Sachs, The Chair (Drew-Leacock); Showman (Maysles Brothers); Chronique d'un Eté (Rouch-Moris); Les Inconnus de la Terre and Regard sur la Folie (Mario Ruspoli); Le Joli Mai (Chris

Marker); <u>Pour la Suite du Monde</u> (Michel Brault). For more details see Appendix.

[17]Joseph V. Mascelli, A. S. C. (comp. and ed.), <u>American Cinematographer Manual</u> (second edition, Hollywood: American Society of Cinematographers, 1966), p. 475.

[18]Ruspoli, <u>op. cit.</u>

[19]<u>Eclair Corporation of America Manual</u>, <u>op. cit.</u>

PART VI:

CONCLUSION

CHAPTER XIII

THE END OR THE WAY?

The pioneers and practitioners of cinéma vérité regard this style as the one that can free cinema from traditional restrictions, liberate it, and lift it into the realm of art and truth. Such a claim in its totality is unrealistic, since cinema is a mass medium of communication, nationally and internationally. Cinéma vérité style appears to be under a compulsion to present a "reality" and "truth" which should be accepted universally. Understandably it has failed to do so, because what is real and true in one culture may be somewhat unreal and untrue in another. For centuries philosophers and other thinkers have tried to find a universal definition of truth, but no one has yet defined the term in a manner acceptable to all.

Cinéma vérité, therefore, as a cinematic style, is closely linked to a given time, place, and set of customs. At best it can reflect a reality in a certain culture, fully appreciable only within the context of that culture--a limitation that is far more relevant to this style than to other cinematic approaches. Great fiction films made in Hollywood have been enjoyed by millions of non-Americans all over the world, but one wonders how many non-Americans would appreciate an American cinéma vérité film such as The Chair or A Time for Burning. This fact seems to preclude any world-wide application of this style and supplies the key to interpreting and evaluating the whole cinéma vérité movement.

The primary concern of cinéma vérité, as was discussed in previous chapters, is that of presenting "truth"-- a truth which cinematically works best when it shows the conflict of man in his society. Each society, however, may tend to conclude erroneously that its basic attitudes and values are universal truths. As the relatively recent science of cultural anthropology has shown, these attitudes and values

are not always readily understood by another society that
has its own particular position. The appreciation of cinéma
vérité films is thus limited in large part to the particular
society in which the film-maker finds his subject matter.
This is not to say that everyone within that society will appreciate a particular film, but there is much greater likeli-
hood of finding an audience within that society than outside
of it. In other words, the appreciation of truth and reality
in its purest form which is advocated by cinéma vérité practitioners is not just a problem of talent or the individual genius of a film-maker; it is basically a problem of the limitations that a cultural sphere imposes on the minds of people.

It is for these reasons that philosophical clashes have
risen among the main proponents of the cinéma vérité movement. Each has dogmatically asserted that his approach best
presents the truth and exemplifies the finest in cinéma vérité
film-making, but, as observed in previous chapters, each
school reflects its own nationalistic interpretations of the
reality and truth. Leacock and Rouch both believe that the
drama most worthy of recording is that of real life (man
against his environment), but they are at loggerheads on the
whole subject of the approach to cinéma vérité--probably because each is trying to portray his own culture basically for
his own culture. Their sharp exchanges of opinion at the
Lyon conference may be explained by their different national
and cultural backgrounds. The individual style of each is a
reflection not only of his personality--and cinéma vérité
probably reflects the personality of its author more faithfully
than any other style of film-making--but also of the society
of which he is a part.

The American cinéma vérité films have been called
cinema of behavior, the disclosing of a character through observing him in his own environment; but such observation
reveals the American man rather than the universal man.
In Leacock's films, for example, the people and situations
are all American, and the American propensity for champions
and furious activity is clearly evident. Perhaps the real
reason Nehru did not work is that Leacock expected to find
a story similar to that of Kennedy in Primary, but could not
create an American champion out of an oriental statesman
whose culture he did not fully understand. The French, on
the other hand, seek truth through dialectics and introspective
analysis, intensive discussion and intimate personal inter-
action--a predisposition clearly evident in the films of Rouch
and Marker. Activity without such discussion has little mean-

ing for the French cinéma vérité film-makers. And, thus,
a cinéma vérité film made in France may have little meaning
for an American audience that is not habitually familiar with
cultural values and behavior patterns of the French people,
and vice versa.

Cinéma vérité has probably been divided into two main
schools because the majority of its exponents are from two
cultures--French and Anglo-Saxon. It is worthy of notice
that a film like Pour la Suite du Monde[1] ("For Posterity")*
by Michel Brault is a mixture of the two cultures (Anglo-
Saxon and French influence in the Canadian culture)--and as
such has been of interest to audiences from both cultures.

The importance and impact of this film, which represents a middle-of-the-road application of cinéma vérité
philosophies and techniques, may be more broadly felt than
that of films made by the fundamentalists who have determined to nurture their specific prejudices. Perhaps the future of cinéma vérité lies partly in this type of application.

One more problem in the cross-cultural communication
of cinéma vérité must be mentioned in passing: the age-old
problem of language. Feature and documentary films of one
language can be successfully dubbed into another language,
keeping much of their flavor. However, dubbing or simultaneous translation of cinéma vérité films to another language
not only loses the film's effectiveness, but is contrary to
the whole theory of presenting the truth as it happened. The
exponents of cinéma vérité seem unanimously in agreement
that in a film of this style it is the spoken word rather than
the visual image that controls. For example, Moi, un Noir
or Le Joli Mai will sacrifice much of its aural beauty and
depth of meaning to non-French speaking audiences. In the
same manner, The Chair and Showman lose much in non-
English speaking countries.

Regardless of the cultural limitations and the language

---

*This full-length film was shot in 16mm and enlarged to
35mm for commercial distribution. It recounts all that happened on the Ile aux Coudres in the St. Lawrence River when
the inhabitants decided to resume fishing for white porpoises
(belugas) after an interruption of 30 years. It is a highly
interesting study of everyday commercial life with the absorb-
ing problem of catching white porpoises in order to sell them
alive to an American aquarium.

Above and opposite, photos from POUR LA SUITE DU MONDE. Courtesy of the National Film Board of Canada.

barrier of cinéma vérité films and the fact that such films
do not present a universal truth, each film made with hones-
ty, technical skill and sensitivity has its usefulness and its
appreciative audience. But the real value of cinéma vérité
becomes apparent when one ceases to consider it as an end
in itself. Its true importance lies not in its variously interpreted doctrines, but in the style itself, which has penetrated
all modes of film-making in the last two decades. It has of-
fered new freedom to film-makers of all cultures, removing
traditional restrictions of massive equipment, ponderous production arrangements, and prohibitive costs. It has brought
new authenticity in cinema. It has liberated it and brought
it closer to life itself. Cinéma vérité is a style that can be
reasonably adapted by any film-maker to his personal and
cultural needs of expression.

Outlets for pure cinéma vérité films are still limited,
but new films are being produced and shown on college cam-
puses, out-of-the-way movie houses, and infrequently on television. The networks, which have tended to dominate productions they finance, are slowly recognizing the effectiveness of this style. The 12-part television series, An American Family, made a few years ago by WNET in Santa Bar-
bara, California, may be considered an experiment in cinéma
vérité. Some critics of this series, which depicted the daily
life of a family made up of a husband, wife and five teenagers,
saw, in the dramatic revelation of the camera, symptoms of
the decline of American family life. Others thought of the
series only as showing the decline of one particular American
family, rather than as presenting a "national truth." Margaret Mead, eminent anthropologist, hailed the series as "the
most important event in human thought since the invention of
the novel."[2]

Cinéma vérité has already exerted considerable influence on other forms of film-making: it has freed conventional cinema from many long-standing restrictions of style
and method, and by developing new aesthetic and technical
approaches has added new dimensions to both theatrical and
documentary film production. Many films utilizing this style
in varying degrees have already won important awards and
wide critical acclaim as well as public acceptance. David
Sawyer's Other Voices (1969), dealing with rehabilitation of
four mental patients, has won an Academy Award nomination.
Donn Alan Pennebaker's Monterey Pop, about the 1967 music
festival at Monterey, California, has proven highly popular
with different audiences; his Don't Look Back, the story of

Bob Dylan's British tour, has been successfully received nationwide. Robert Drew's Children Were Watching and Crisis: Behind a Presidential Commitment have received some acclaim, and Frank Simon's The Queen has had successful bookings in many movie theaters across the country. Birth and Death by Arthur and Evelyn Farron, which is the story of a young couple who are expecting a baby and a lonely old man who is dying but afraid of death, was turned down by many networks, but was widely praised when shown on public broadcasting stations in 1969.

François Truffaut's L'argent de Poche ("Pocket Money") is a film about children, from their perspective, which has won acclaim both in Europe and the United States. The film, shown in 1977, is a rare work of Truffaut's, which depicts many adventures of children in terms of their own experiences and aspirations. With a cast of 200 children, none of them professional actors, the film is a living example of cinéma vérité influence and penetration into feature film production.

Many camera techniques of cinéma vérité style which were totally unacceptable some 20 years ago are being freely utilized in documentary as well as feature films. A well-known example in feature films is the restaurant scene in A Man and a Woman, the Academy Award winner of 1968. An instance in the field of documentary is certain sequences from The Investor and the Marketplace (1969), a 22-minute color film about the stock exchange, directed by Hans Mandell.

Tomorrow Entertainment has made a number of films for television (using certain of the cinéma vérité techniques) including: The Autobiography of Jane Pittman, filmed on the plantation and former slave houses in Louisiana; The Glass House, shot entirely within a prison; A War of Children, filmed in Northern Ireland, and Larry, made entirely inside a state mental hospital.

Roger Gimbel, vice president in charge of production, has been quoted as saying, "There's a quality in location shooting that no writer can write into a script and that no director can direct an actor toward. The actors and the crew get the feel of being in a prison, or of being near the conflict of Northern Ireland. You hear the real screams in a mental hospital. It's something no director can impart."[3]

And so, cinéma vérité, or at least its philosophy of

truthfulness, has slowly become an integral part of film-making. It did not replace the conventional cinema as many proponents preached or wished it to do, but has become a part of it, bringing new freedom and freshness of expression into it. It destroyed some of the conventions of the traditional cinema while at the same time releasing film-making for new growth just as the invention of photography relieved painting from some of its pictorial reproduction function, setting it free to pursue new avenues to artistic goals.

The cinematic meshing of reality with dramatic material has a tremendous revitalizing potential for the future of film-making. As Chris Marker admirably stated, "Vérité n'êst pas le but, mais peut-etre la route"--vérité is not the end, but perhaps it is the way.

NOTES

[1] 16mm, B and W, feature length. Cameras: Arriflex and Auricon. Recorder: Nagra. Synchronization system: Pilot-guided. Photographed by Michel Brault. Sound-men: Marcel Carrière, Michel Perraut. Co-Directors: Michel Brault and Michel Perraut.

[2] Rhoda Amon, "Divorced Wife of 'Family' Series Tells Her Side," Lansing State Journal, April 9, 1974.

[3] "On-the-Spot Realism Brings Acclaim to Television Films," a national wire release to Lansing State Journal, published April 26, 1974.

APPENDIX

SELECTED LIST OF CINEMA VERITE FILMS

The following list of films, compiled from various sources, most notably from Ruspoli's UNESCO report, [1] represents films particularly characteristic of, and important to, the cinéma vérité style and movement.

Some of the films listed have been discussed in the body of the book; others, listed but not discussed, are the work of film-makers whose approaches have been mentioned briefly. The list makes no pretense of including all important films made in this style, nor those films which in varying degree resemble cinéma vérité. Readers interested in additional information on such films may refer to Luc de Heusch's survey[2] or similar publications.

United States of America

PRIMARY (1960)
        16mm, B & W. Length 54 minutes. Camera: Auricon. Recorder: Nagra. Synchronization system: Accutron. Photographed by: Richard Leacock, Donn Alan Pennebaker, Albert Maysles, Terry Filgate. Produced by: Robert Drew.

A candid study of Senators John Kennedy and Hubert Humphrey in their now historic contest in the 1960 Wisconsin primary election. Two teams equipped with synchronization units continually followed the two candidates, but without intervening, and photographed some remarkably revealing pictorial glimpses of them, their wives, and their campaign entourage. Strongly Vertovian in character and highly objective in its treatment, this outstanding reportage film avoids propaganda of any kind, draws no moral, and follows no "plot" other than the chronology of the events which led to Kennedy's winning the election. The audio-visual operation, using prototype equipment for the first time, was carried out under particularly difficult conditions and was an astonishing feat.

EDDIE SACHS (1959-60-61)
(Original title "On the Pole")
16mm, B & W and color, full length. Camera: Auricon. Recorder: Nagra. Synchronization system: Pilot-guided and Accutron. Photographed by: Richard Leacock, Albert Maysles, Donn Alan Pennebaker.

Within the framework of a series on the American male, which had already included "X-15 Pilot," the camera now follows the motor-racing champion Eddie Sachs over a period of three consecutive years as he seeks to win the famous Indianapolis race. For the third time running, he fails to win in 1961 but comes in second. The film begins in black and white and then switches to color. It gives a fascinating glimpse of the atmosphere of American sport and the ways of American sportsmen. Outstanding aspects are the richness of the live sound and the moments of genuine excitement and suspense resulting from actual occurrences.

THE CHAIR (1962)
16mm, B & W, 72 minutes. Camera: Auricon. Recorders: Nagra and Stellavox. Synchronization system: Accutron. Photographed by: Richard Leacock, Donn Alan Pennebaker. Directed by: Gregory Shuker. Produced by: Robert Drew.

In this film two cinéma vérité teams, one consisting of Leacock/Drew and one Pennebaker/Shuker, penetrate into a human drama which raises the question of the American legal system in relation to the death penalty. The two teams succeed in capturing the most dramatic moments preceding the execution of a condemned black man named Paul Crump. The life of the condemned man during the five days before the execution date, the anguish of the executioner who is his friend, the lawyer's efforts, the court in session are dramatically captured. Finally, the State Governor commutes the sentence to life imprisonment. A formidable indictment of capital punishment, based solely on a strictly chronological record of authentic facts photographed from life.

NEHRU (1963)
16mm, B & W, 60 minutes. Camera: Auricon. Re-

corder: Nagra. Synchronization system: Accutron. Photographed by: Richard Leacock. Assisted by: Robert Drew, Gregory Shuker.

A film showing 15 days in the life of Nehru, the late Prime Minister of India, during the Indian election.

HAPPY MOTHER'S DAY (1963-64)
(Formerly called "The Fischer Quintuplets")
16mm, B & W. Camera: Auricon. Recorder: Nagra. Synchronization system: Accutron. Photographed by: Richard Leacock, Donn Alan Pennebaker. Produced by: Drew Associates.

A film ostensibly about the events surrounding the birth of the famous Fischer quintuplets. The Saturday Evening Post commissioned the film and wanted it to be one hour long. A 60-minute film was made but later Drew Associates bought the film from them and cut it to a shorter length. However, due to some legal complications, two prints of everything shot had to be given to ABC, from which they made a 30-minute film, which was shown on television.

SHOWMAN (1962)
16mm, B & W, 53 minutes. Camera: Auricon. Recorder: Nagra Neo-Pilot. Synchronization system: Accutron. Photographed by: Albert Maysles. Sounded and edited by: David Maysles.

Al Maysles' amazing camera follows the vicissitudes which accompany the conclusion of a big film and publicity deal. Joe Levine, a well-known and typical American big businessman, meets Sophia Loren at the Cannes Festival. She is the star of a production which he is promoting. Scenes from the life of a showman, in which the world of the American big businessman is examined objectively, intelligently and sincerely, by the use of absolutely authentic elements filmed on the spot.

TIME FOR BURNING (1966)
16mm, B & W, 58 minutes. Camera: Eclair NPR. Recorder: Nagra. Photographed by: William C. Jersey. Jr. Produced by: The Lutheran Film Associates.

The true story of the step-by-step ordeal of the Augustana Lutheran Church in Omaha, Nebraska, is presented when a modest plan for improving race relations with nearby Negro churches meets stiff resistance from white parishioners. The film chronicles the controversy that ensued among church leaders, along with the resultant resignation of the pastor, and gives startling insight into the honest feelings of those involved.

France

CHRONIQUE D'UN ETE ("Summer Story"; 1961)
16mm, B & W, feature length. Camera: Coutant-Mathot KMT. Recorders: Nagra Neo-Pilot and Perfectone. Synchronization system: Pilot-guided. Photographed by: Michel Brault, Roger Morillère, Raoul Coutard, Jean-Jacques Tarbes. Edited by: Jean Ravel, Nina Baratier, Françoise Colin. Directed by: Jean Rouch, Edgar Morin.

This full-length feature, initially 21 hours long and later cut to one hour and forty-five minutes, was photographed in 16mm and enlarged to 35mm for theatrical release. The film concerns the lives of Parisians in 1961; it begins by showing the reactions of passersby in Paris to the question, "Are you happy?" and goes on interviewing people in great detail about their lives. Finally it shows their reactions on viewing the record of their interview and discussion.

LA PUNITION ("The Punishment"; 1963)
16mm, B & W, feature length. Camera: Coutant-Mathot KMT. Photographed by: Michel Brault, Roger Morillère, George Dufaux. Directed by: Jean Rouch. Players: Nadine Ballot, Jean-Marc Simon, Jean-Claude Darnel, Modeste Landry.

This film, shot in 1960 and released in 1963, is the story of one day in Nadine Ballot's life when, because of tardiness, she is refused admittance for the day to the school where she is studying philosophy. Afraid of going home, she wanders around in Paris and meets three people, a student who declares himself to be in love with her and then leaves her with a middle-aged engineer who asks her to go home with him and a black man acquaintance.

LES INCONNUS DE LA TERRE ("The Unknown of the Earth"; 1961)
16mm, B & W, medium length. Camera: Coutant-Mathot KMT. Recorders: Nagra Neo-Pilot and Perfectone. Synchronization system: Pilot-guided. Photographed by: Michel Brault, Roger Morillère. Sound-men: Roger Morillère, Danielle Tessier. Assistant: Dolores Grassian. Editors: Jean Ravel, Mario Ruspoli. Directed by: Mario Ruspoli

This film was shot on 16mm and enlarged to 35mm. It is a direct-cinema survey of the living conditions of a section of the rural population in the Lozère, grappling with the problems of isolation, underpopulation and the difficulty of achieving adequate production.

REGARD SUR LA FOLIE ("A Look at Madness"; 1961)
16mm, B & W, medium length. Cameras: Coutant-Mathot KMT, Arriflex. Recorder: Nagra. Synchronization system: Pilot-guided. Photographed by: Michel Brault, Roger Morillère, Mario Ruspoli. Sound-men: D. Tessier, D. Grassian, R. Morillère. Editors: Henri Colpi, Henri Lanoe, Jacqueline Meppiel. Directed by: Mario Ruspoli.

Aspects of life in a psychiatric hospital (Saint-Alban, Lozère). Endeavors to communicate the "feeling of madness." Various activities of patients' groups: occupational therapy, psychotherapy, sociotherapy, ending with the hospital's annual celebration.

LE JOLI MAI ("Pretty May"; 1963)
16mm, B & W, full length. Cameras: Coutant-Mathot KMT, Arriflex. Recorder: Perfectone, Nagra. Synchronization system: Pilot-guided. Photographed by: Pierre Lhomme, Denis Clairval. Assistant: Etienne Becker. Sound-man: Antoine Bonfanti. Editor: Eva Zora. Director: Chris Marker.

In the full-length three-hour version, shot in 16mm and enlarged to 35mm, this film achieved the dimension of a masterpiece of sociological investigation into the various problems that Parisians had to face on the eve of the Algerian war. Unique in its field and bearing the imprint of its makers' personalities, it is at once a statement, an analysis, and an indictment. Unfortunately, it was not possible to show it commercially in its full-length version, and the director was compelled to make certain cuts. Its present running time represents a reduction of one hour, and what has been removed was as rich in interest as the rest.

ADIEU PHILIPPINE ("Goodby Philippine"; 1963)
    Length 1 hour 45 minutes. Directed by: Jacques Rozier. Produced by: Carlo Ponti.

    This film is the story of a television cable boy in Paris who is called off to military service at the time of the Algerian war. Before joining the service he meets two girls who are great friends and takes them both out alternately in Paris, spends his holiday with them in Corsica and has an affair with each of them before going off to Algeria, thus making the two girls great enemies. Although this is a feature film, Rozier uses all the cinéma vérité techniques--nonactors, improvised technique, etc.

Canada

POUR LA SUITE DU MONDE ("For Posterity"; 1963)
    16mm, B & W, feature length. Cameras: Arriflex and Auricon. Recorder: Nagra. Synchronization system: Pilot-guided. Photographed by: Michel Brault. Sound-men: Marcel Carrière, Michel Perraut. Co-directors: Michel Brault, Michel Perraut.

    This full-length film was shot in 16mm and enlarged to 35mm for commercial distribution. It recounts all that happened on the Ile aux Coudres in the St. Lawrence River when the inhabitants decided to resume fishing for white porpoises (belugas) after an interruption of 30 years. A highly interesting study of everyday commercial life in a small community of peasant-fishermen, faced with the absorbing problem of catching white porpoises in order to sell them alive to an American aquarium.

NOTES

    [1]Mario Ruspoli, "Towards a New Film Technique in the Developing Countries. The Light-Weight Synchronized Cinematographic Unit" (UNESCO Report to Second Beirut Round-Table on "Arab Cinema and Culture," October 28-30,

1963. W. S. /1063. 1 (CUA). Paris: 1964. Translated from the French. Mimeographed.

[2]Luc de Heusch, The Cinema and Social Science, A Survey of Ethnographic and Sociological Films (UNESCO Reports and Papers in the Social Sciences, No. 16, 1962. SS. 62. XV. 16A. Paris, 1962).

BIBLIOGRAPHY

ENGLISH

Books

Armes, Roy. French Cinema since 1946. Vol. I: The
    Great Tradition. Amsterdam: Drukkerijen vh., Eller-
    man Harms NV, 1966.

_____. French Cinema since 1946. Vol. II: The
    Personal Style. Amsterdam: Drukkerijen vh. Eller-
    man Harms NV, 1966.

Barnouw, Erik. Documentary, a History of the Non-Fiction
    Films. New York: Oxford University Press, 1974.

Bleum, A. William. Documentary in American Television.
    New York: Hastings House, 1965.

_____, and Manvell, Roger, eds. Television, the
    Creative Experience--A Survey of Anglo-American
    Progress. New York: Hastings House, 1967.

Flaherty, Frances Hubbard. The Odyssey of a Film-Maker,
    Robert Flaherty's Story. Urbana, Illinois: Beta Phi
    Mu, 1960.

Lawson, John Howard. Film, the Creative Process. 2d ed.
    New York: Hill and Wang, 1964.

Manvell, Roger. New Cinema in Europe. New York: E. P.
    Dutton & Co., Inc., 1966.

Mascelli, Joseph V., A.S.C., comp. and ed. American
    Cinematographer Manual. 2d ed. Hollywood: Amer-
    ican Society of Cinematographers, 1966.

Robinson, David. The History of World Cinema. New York: Stein and Day, 1973.

Rotha, Paul, and additional section by Richard Griffith. The Film Till Now, a Survey of World Cinema. London: Spring Books, 1967.

Souto, H. Mario Raimondo. The Technique of the Motion Picture Camera, edited by Raymond Spottiswoode. New York: Communication Arts Books, Hastings House, 1967.

Swallow, Norman. Factual Television. New York: Hastings House, 1966.

Periodicals

Alimendros, Nestor. "Neorealist Cinematography," Film Culture, No. 20 (October 1959), 39-43.

Arnheim, Rudolf. "Free Cinema II," Film Culture, IV, No. 2 (17) (February 1958), 11.

Bachmann, Gideon. "The Frontiers of Realist Cinema: The Work of Ricky Leacock (from an interview conducted by Gideon Bachmann)," Film Culture, Nos. 22-23 (Summer 1961), 12-23.

Barnouw, Erik. "Films of Social Comment," Film Comment, II, No. 1 (Winter 1964), 16, 17.

Bazin, André. "Cinema and Television, Jean Renoir and Roberto Rossellini Interviewed by André Bazin," Sight and Sound, XXVIII, No. 1 (Winter 1958/59), 26-30.

Blue, James. "One Man's Truth, An Interview with Richard Leacock," Film Comment, III, No. 2 (Spring 1965), 16-22.

_____. "Thoughts on Cinéma Vérité and a Discussion with the Maysles Brothers," Film Comment, II, No. 4 (Fall 1965), 22-30.

Breitrose, Henry. "On the Search for the Real Nitty-Gritty: Problems and Possibilities in Cinéma-Vérité" (Three Views on Cinéma-Vérité), Film Quarterly, XVII, No. 4 (Summer 1964), 36-40.

Bronson, Gerald. "The Candid Photography of 'The Fabian Story,'" American Cinematographer (October 1964), 582-584.

C., E. "A Further Note on Technology," Film Quarterly, XVIII, No. 1 (Fall 1964), 33.

Cameron, Ian, and Shivas, Mark. "Cinéma-Vérité," Movie, No. 8 (April 1963), 12-15.

_____. _____. "Interviews (with Richard Leacock, Albert and David Maysles, William Klein, Jean Rouch, Jacques Rozier)," Movie, No. 8 (April 1963), 16-26.

Crawford, Stanley. "From Visionary Gleams to Cinéma-Vérité," Film, No. 40 (1964), 34-39.

Dyer, John. "Renoir and Realism," Sight and Sound, XXIX, No. 3 (Summer 1960), 130-135.

Graham, Peter. "Cinéma-Vérité in France" (Three Views on Cinéma-Vérité), Film Quarterly, XVII, No. 4 (Summer 1964), 30-36.

Gray, Paul. "Cinéma Vérité--An Interview with Barbet Schroeder," tdr--Tulane Drama Review, XI, No. 1 (T33) (Fall 1966), 130-132.

Haleff, Maxine. "The Maysles Brothers and 'Direct Cinema,'" Film Comment, II, No. 2 (1964), 19-23.

Hill, Jerome. "Making a Documentary--Albert Schweitzer," Film Culture, No. 2 (12) (1957), 10-12.

Horne, Denis. "The Free Cinema Hoax," Film Journal, No. 17 (April 1961), 103-109.

Jacobs, Lewis. "Free Cinema I," Film Culture, IV, No. 2 (17) (February 1958), 9-11.

Jaffe, Patricia. "Editing Cinéma Vérité," Film Comment, III, No. 3 (Summer 1965), 43-47.

Jersey, William C., Jr. "Some Observations on Cinéma Vérité," Motive, XXVII, No. 2 (November 1966), 11, 12.

_____. "Some Thoughts on Film Technique," <u>Film Comment</u>, II, No. 1 (Winter 1964), 15, 16.

Junker, Howard. "The National Film Board of Canada: After a Quarter Century," <u>Film Quarterly</u>, XVII, No. 2 (Winter 1964-65), 22-29.

Lane, John Francis. "Letter from Rome," <u>Contrast</u>, II, No. 4 (Summer 1963), 259, 260.

Leacock, Richard. "For an Uncontrolled Cinema," <u>Film Culture</u>, Nos. 22/23 (Summer 1961), 23-25.

_____. "Ricky Leacock on 'Stravinsky' Film," <u>Film Culture</u>, No. 42 (Fall 1966), 113.

Lipscomb, James C. "Correspondence and Controversy: Cinéma-Vérité," <u>Film Quarterly</u>, XVIII, No. 2 (Winter 1964-65), 62, 63.

Luft, Herbert G. "Karl Freund," <u>Films in Review</u>, XIV, No. 2 (February 1963), 93-108.

Marcorelles, Louis (interviewing Richard Leacock). "The Deep Well," <u>Contrast</u>, III, No. 5 (Autumn 1964), 246-249.

_____. "Jean-Luc Godard's Half Truths," <u>Film Quarterly</u>, Vol. XVII, No. 3 (Spring 1964), 5.

_____. "Nothing But the Truth," <u>Sight and Sound</u>, XXXII, No. 3 (Summer 1963), 114-117.

"Maysles Brothers," <u>Film Culture</u>, No. 42 (Fall 1966), 114.

Mekas, Jonas. "A Call for a New Generation of Film Makers," <u>Film Culture</u>, No. 19 (January 26, 1959), 1-3.

_____. "Cinema of the New Generation," <u>Film Culture</u>, No. 21 (Summer 1960), 1-20.

_____. "Notes on the New American Cinema," <u>Film Culture</u>, No. 24 (Spring 1962), 6-16.

_____. "Toward a Spontaneous Cinema," <u>Sight and Sound</u>, XXVIII, Nos. 3 and 4 (Summer/Autumn 1959), 118-123.

Rhode, Eric. "Why Neo-Realism Failed," Sight and Sound, XXX, No. 1 (Winter 1960/61), 27-32.

Rogosin, Lionel. "Interpreting Reality (Notes on Esthetics and Practices of Improvisational Acting)," Film Culture, No. 21 (Summer 1960), 20-28.

Sadoul, Georges. "Notes on a New Generation," Sight and Sound, XXVIII, Nos. 3 and 4 (Summer/Autumn 1959), 112-117.

Sarris, Andrew. "The American Cinema," Film Culture, No. 28 (Spring 1963), 1-52.

Siclier, Jacques. "New Wave and French Cinema," Sight and Sound, XXX, No. 3 (Summer 1961), 116-120.

Sipherd, Ray. "The Long Courtship: Films of Social Inquiry for Television," Film Comment, II, No. 1 (Winter 1964), 17-19.

Smith, Hubert. "The University Film Director and Cinéma-Vérité," Journal of the University Film Producers Association, XIX, No. 2 (1967), 58-62.

Tanner, Alain. "Recording Africa," Sight and Sound, Vol. 26 (1) (Summer 1956), 42.

Vertov, Dziga, "The Writings of Dziga Vertov," Film Culture, No. 25 (Summer 1962), 50-65.

Weinberg, Herman, G. "The Man with the Movie Camera," Film Comment, IV, No. 1 (Fall 1966), 40-42.

Young, Colin. "Cinema of Common Sense" (Three Views on Cinéma-Vérité), Film Quarterly, XVII, No. 4 (Summer 1964), 26-40.

Zavattini, Cesare. "Some Ideas on the Cinema," Sight and Sound, XXIII, No. 1 (July/September 1953), 64-69.

Papers and Theses

Clapp, Nicholas Roger. "The Naturalistic Documentary, 1896-1960." Unpublished Master's Thesis, Department of Cinema, University of Southern California, Los Angeles, August 1962.

de Heusch, Luc. The Cinema and Social Science, a Survey of Ethnographic and Sociological Films. UNESCO Reports and Papers in the Social Sciences, No. 16, 1962. SS. 62. XV. 16A. Paris: 1962.

Eclair Corporation of America Manual. Los Angeles: The Corporation, August 1966.

Ruspoli, Mario. "Towards a New Film Technique in the Developing Countries. The Light-Weight Synchronized Cinematographic Unit." UNESCO Report to Second Beirut Round-Table on "Arab Cinema and Culture," October 28-30, 1963. WS/1063. 1 (CUA). Paris: 1964. (Translated from the French.) (Mimeographed.)

Interviews and Letters

Carson and McBride. Interview with William C. Jersey, Jr., March 30, 1967. (Mimeographed.)

Issari, M. Ali. Interview with Herb Stern, Head Legal Department, M. C. A., Inc., March 1967.

Miller, Perry. Interview with Willard Van Dyke, James C. Lipscomb, and William C. Jersey, Jr., May 16, 1967, New York Film Council. (Mimeographed.)

Ruspoli, Mario. Letter to the author, March 26, 1967.

FRENCH

Books

Sadoul, Georges. Histoire d'un Art: Le Cinéma. Paris: Flammarion, 1940.

Periodicals

Barthès, Roland. "Preface to Les Inconnus de la Terre," Artsept, No. 2 (April-June 1963), 76.

Bellour, Raymond. "Les Signes et la Métamorphose," Artsept, No. 2, Le Cinéma et la Vérité (Avril/Juin 1963) 131-138.

_____, et Jean-Louis Leutrat. "Preface," Artsept, No. 2, Le Cinéma et la Vérité (Avril/Juin 1963), 5-7.

Borde, Raymond. "Problemes du Cinéma-Vérité," Positif, Mensuel 49 (Decembre 1962), 1-8.

Bory, Jean-Louis. "Vessies et Lanternes" ("The Moon Is Made of Green Cheese"), Artsept, No. 2 (April-June 1963), 55-60.

Bringuier, Jean-Claude. "Libres Propos sur le Cinéma-Vérité," Cahiers du Cinéma, XXV, No. 145 (Juillet 1963), 14-17.

Delahaye, Michel. "La Chasse a l'I," Cahiers du Cinéma, XXV, No. 146 (Aout 1963), 5-17.

"Dictionnaire Partiel et Partial d'un Nouveau Cinéma Français," Positif, Mensuel 46 (Juin 1962), 19-38.

"Entretien avec Jean Rouch," Image et Son, No. 173 (Mai 1964), 44-45.

"Entretien avec Mario Ruspoli," Image et Son, No. 173 (Mai 1964), 46-54.

Gautheir, Claude. "Adieu Philippine," Cinéma 62, No. 64 (Mars 1962), 59-64.

Goldman, Lucien. "Cinema and Sociology; Consideration of A Summer Chronicle," Artsept, No. 2 (April-June 1963), p. 5 of translation.

Jambon, Alexis, ed. Artsept, No. 2, Le Cinéma et la Vérité (Avril/Juin 1963) 1-169.

Julien, Claude. "A Man in a Crowd," Artsept, No. 2 (April-June 1963), 45-48.

Labarthe, André S., et Louis Marcorelles. "Entretien avec Robert Drew et Richard Leacock," Cahiers du Cinéma, XXIV, No. 140 (Fevrier 1963), 18-25.

Leacock, Richard. "La Camera Passe-Partout," Cahiers du Cinéma, XVI, No. 94 (Avril 1959), 37-38.

Marcorelles, Louis. "Le Cinéma Direct Nord Américain,"

Image et Son, No. 183 (Avril 1965), 47-54.

_____. "L'Expérience Leacock," Cahiers du Ciné-
ma, XXIV, No. 140 (Fevrier 1963), 11-17.

_____. "La Foire aux Vérités," Cahiers du Ciné-
ma, XXIV, No. 140 (Fevrier 1963), 26-34.

Prédal, René. "A Chacun sa Vérité," Jeune Cinéma, No. 15
(Mai 1966), 23-25.

Rohmer, Eric, et Louis Marcorelles. "Entretien avec Jean
Rouch," Cahiers du Cinéma, XXIV, No. 144 (Juin
1963), 1-22.

Rozier, Jacques. "Adieu Philippine," Artsept, No. 3
(Octobre-Decembre 1963), 61-66.

_____. "Adieu Philippine," L'Avant Scène du Cin-
éma, No. 31 (Novembre 15, 1963) 47.

Sadoul, Georges. "Actualité de Dziga Vertov," Cahiers du
Cinéma, XXIV, No. 144 (Juin 1963), 23-31.

_____. "Bio-Filmographie de Dziga Vertov,"
Cahiers du Cinéma, XXV, No. 146 (Aôut 1963), 21-
29.

_____. "Dziga Vertov," Artsept, No. 2, Le Ciné-
ma et la Vérité (Avril/Juin 1963) 18-19.

"Table-Ronde: Cinéma-Vérité," Objectif (Aôut 1963) 35-38.

"Table-Ronde: Festival de Tours en Collaboration avec
l'U. N. E. S. C. O. ," Image et Son, No. 160 (Mars
1963), 5-17.

Thirard, Paul-Louis. "Drew, Leacock and Company," Artsept, No. 2 (April-June 1963), 44.

Vertov, Dziga. "Dziga Vertov--Kinoks-Révolution II," Cahiers
du Cinéma, XXV, No. 146 (Aôut 1963), 18-20.

_____. "Fragments," Artsept, No. 2, Le Cinéma
et la Vérité (Avril/June 1963), 19-20.

Vrasplokh, Jizn. "Improvisation of Life," Cahiers du Cinéma, No. 144 (June 1963), p. 24 of translation.

Papers

de Heusch, Luc. "The Cinema and Social Science: A Survey of Ethnographic and Sociological Films," United Nations Educational, Scientific and Cultural Organization, No. 16, 1962. [Also listed under English.]

ITALIAN

Periodicals

Antonioni, Michelangelo. "Infrarosso--La Realtà e il Cinema-Diretto," Cinema Nuovo, XIII, No. 167 (Gennaio-Febbraio 1964), 8-10.

Apra, Adriano, Maurizio Ponzi, and Stefano Roncoroni. "Intervista con Jacques Rozier," Filmcritica, No. 150 (Ottobre 1964), 517-529.

Bruno, Edoardo. "Prospettive del Cinema Diretto in Relazione al Linguaggio Filmico," Filmcritica, XVII, No. 163 (Gennaio 1966), 3-7.

Casiraghi, Ugo. "La Rivincita del Cine Verità," La Fiera del Cinema (Luglio 1963), 18-31.

Collet, Jean. "I Due Volti del Cinéma-Vérità," Cine Forum, No. 26 (Giugno 1963), 525-538.

Gregoricchio, Gianni. "Verità e Mistificazione del Cinema-Verita," Cine Forum, No. 43 (Marzo 1965), 225-236.

May, Renato. "Dal Cinema al Cinema-Verità," Bianco e Nero, XXV, Nos. 4-5 (Aprile-Maggio 1964), 1-15.

Natta, Enzo. "Pro e Contro il Cinéma Vérité," Rivista del Cinematografo (Novembre 1963), 418-421.

Plebe, Armando. "Il 'Cinema-Verita': Ragioni e Pericoli di Una Moda," Filmcritica, XIV, No. 137 (Settembre 1963), 511-519.

Ruspoli, Mario. "Cinema-Direct," Filmselezione, No. 15-
16 (1963), 73-77.

_____. "Esperience nel Cinema e nella Televisione,
Il Gruppo Sincrono Leger," Filmselezione, Nos. 19-20
(1963), 113-121.

Sasso, Rino dal. "Umberto Barbaro e la Critica," Filmcritica, XVI, No. 155 (Marzo 1965), 147-151.

Solaroli, Libero. "I Tre 'Impegni' di Barbaro," Filmcritica,
XVI, No. 155 (Marzo 1965), 152-158.

Tomasino, Renato. "Il Concetto di Collaborazione in Barbaro," Filmcritica XVI, No. 155 (Marzo 1965), 159-
161.

CZECH

Periodicals

Svanda, Pavel. "Film Pravda a Naš Divăk," Film a Doba,
XI, No. 1 (Leden 1965), 26-31.

GERMAN

Periodicals

"'Cinéma-Vérité'-Das Leben, Wie Es Ist?" Filmkritik,
(Maerz 1964), 116-128.

Gregor, Ulrich. "Leacock oder Das Kino der Physiker--
Ulrich Gregor im Gespräech mit dem amerikanischen
Filmaker Richard Leacock," Film, 4. Jahrgang,
Heft 1 (Januar 1966), 14-19.

Ladiges, P. M. "Richard Leacocks Experiment mit der
Wirklichkeit: Eine Einfuehrung in das 'Cinema-
Verite,'" Film, 1. Jahrgang, Heft 3 (August/Septem-
ber 1963), 10-11.

Partzsch, Klaus. "Die Ungekuerzte Wirklichkeit," Film, 3.
Jahrgang, Heft 6 (Juni 1965), 19-20.

Ruspoli, Mario. "Wie Filmt Man Wahrheit, Von der 'Kino-Prawda' bis zum 'Cinéma-Vérité,'" Film, 3. Jahrgang, Heft 2 (Februar 1965), 46-48.

Von Thuena, Ulrich. "Die Schoenheit des Alltaeglichen," Film, 1. Jahrgang, Heft 1 (April/Mai 1963), 24-25.

DANISH

Periodicals

Kovacs, Yves. "Hvad er Cinéma Vérité?" Kosmorama, No. 65 (Februar 1964), 100-108.

PORTUGUESE

Periodicals

Liniers, Jean. "Cinema Verdade," Filme (Dezembro 1963), 17-20.

Monteiro, Marialva P., and Ronaldo F. Monteiro. "O Cinema-Verdade," R. C. Cinemat, No. 35 (1963), 51-62.

Rouch, Jean. "O que é o Cinema-Verdade, A Propósito de 'Chronique d'un Eté,'" Celuloide, V, No. 61 (Janeiro 1963), 4-6.

_____, and Morin, Edgar. "O que é o Cinema-Verdade," Celuloide, V, No. 62 (Fevereiro 1963), 4-6.

RUSSIAN

Periodicals

Fradkin, G. "Is Richard Leacock Correct?" Iskusstvo Kino No. 11 (1965), 24-25.

SPANISH

Periodicals

C., J. "Cinéma Vérité," Film Ideal, No. 131 (Noviembre 1, 1963), 650-652.

SWEDISH

Periodicals

Rouch, Jean. "Afrika vaknar," Vilm Rutan, No. 1 (1966), 62-67.

Sima, Jonas. "Cinema Direct och Mario Ruspoli," Chaplin 62, VIII, No. 2 (Februari 1966), 66.

_____. "Cinéma Vérité," Chaplin 46, VI, No. 4 (April 1964), 132-140.

ADDENDUM

Amon, Rhoda. "Divorced Wife of 'Family' Series Tells Her Side," Lansing State Journal, (April 9, 1974).

Dort, Bernard. "Un Cinéma de la description." Artsept No. 2, Le Cinéma et la Vérité, (Avril/Juin 1963) 125-130.

Issari, M. Ali and Doris A. Paul. Interview with Kenneth Richter, Lansing, Mich. April 28, 1979.

MacFadden, Patrick. "Gimme Shelter," Film Society Review, Vol. 6, No. 3 (1970), 39-42.

"On-the-Spot Realism Brings Acclaim to Television Films," a national wire release to Lansing State Journal, April 26, 1974.

"The Technology," Film Quarterly, xvii, No. 4 (Summer 1964) 24-25.

INDEX

Adieu Philippine (Goodby Philippine) 50, 119, 120, 121, 184
American Broadcasting Company 94
American Broadcasting Company TV News 60
An American Family 176
Anderson, Lindsay 7, 52, 55, 56
Angénieux, Pierre 159
Antonioni, Michelangelo 9, 41
L'argent de Poche (Pocket Money) 177
Armistarco, Guido 11
Armes, Roy 8, 15, 61, 119, 122, 124
Arnheim, Rudolph 54, 55
Les Astronautes 122
Astruc, Alexandre 18
Auschwitz, the Last Stage 41
Autant-Lara, Claude 41
The Autobiography of Jane Pittman 177

Baratier, Nina 182
Bardot, Brigitte 47
Barthes, Roland 117
La Bataille du Rail (Railway Battle) 41
Bazin, André 60, 149
Becker, Etienne 118, 183
Bellour, Raymond 122, 124
Belmondo, Jean-Paul 49
Berlin die Symphonie einer Grosstadt (Berlin, Symphony of a Big City) 68
Bernstein, Leonard 86
Berthiat 158, 159
The Bicycle Thief 42, 44
Birth and Death 177
Bitzer, Billy 68
Bleum, A. William 7, 86, 89, 90, 91, 101
Blue, James 12, 14, 38, 89, 95, 105, 127, 133, 134
Blue Jeans 119

Bonfanti, Antoine 118, 183
Borde, Raymond 11, 116
Borowczyk, Walerian 122
Bory, Jean-Louis 79
Braine, John 56
Brault, Michel 7, 72, 74, 117, 154, 155, 165, 173, 182, 183, 184
Breathless 48, 49
Breitrose, Henry 12
Bringuier, Jean-Claude 7, 109
British Film Institute 54
Bruno, Edoardo 49
Buffet, Bernard 122

Cahiers du Cinema 46, 47, 52, 77
Cameron, Ian A. 120, 152
Camus, Marcel 47
Canadian Broadcasting Company 17
Candid-Eye 7
Carrière, Marcel 184
Cartier-Bresson, Henri 133
Cassavetes, John 140
Cast the First Stone 60
Chabrol, Claude 46, 47
The Chair 89, 90, 91, 92, 93, 97, 106, 154, 163, 171, 173, 180
Charlotte and Her Jules 49
Chasse à l'Hippopotame (Hippopotamus Hunt) 67, 68
Chevalier, Maurice 61
The Children Were Watching 89, 177
Chronique d'un Eté (A Summer Chronicle) 6, 50, 72, 73, 74, 75, 76, 109, 118, 122, 123, 140, 155, 162, 165, 182
Cimetière dans la Falaise 69
Cine-Eye 6, 18, 24, 25, 26, 27, 28, 30, 31
Cine-Radio 29
Cinema d'auteurs 44
Cinema of Behavior 7
Cinema of Common Sense 7
Clairval, Denis 183
Clayton, Jack 56
Clément, René 41
Clore, Leon 54
Close-Up 60
Colin, Françoise 182
Colpi, Henri 183
Columbia Broadcasting System 60

Come Back, Africa 138, 139
Constantine, Eddie 71
Coutant, André 7, 155, 156
Coutard, Raoul 182
Cowie, Peter 13
Crisis: Behind a Presidential Commitment 177
Cuba Si 50, 87, 122, 123

Description d'un Combat 122
de Heusch, Luc 36, 69, 87, 139, 179
de Sica, Vittoria 41, 42, 43, 44, 125
Le Diable Corps 41
Direct Cinema 7, 8, 50, 115, 116, 117, 119, 152, 154
Direct Shooting 7
Dr. Jekyll and Mr. Hyde 60
Don't Look Back 176
Doolittle, Jimmy 61
Dort, Bernard 85
Dovzhenko 23
Drew, Robert 6, 7, 10, 16, 85, 86, 87, 88, 89, 91, 94,
    105, 106, 108, 124, 163, 177, 179, 180, 181
Drew Associates 91, 92, 93, 94, 96, 97, 124, 125, 153,
    154, 181
Dufaux, George 182
Dylan, Bob 177

Eclair Camera 7
Eddie Sachs at Indianapolis (originally called On the Pole)
    89, 92, 93, 154, 163, 180
Eisenstein, Sergei 9, 23
Elephant Boy 36
Every Day Except Christmas 54, 55

Fabbretti, Nazareno 10
Farron, Arthur 177
Farron, Evelyn 177
Fellini 41
Une Femme Est Une Femme (A Woman Is a Woman) 49
Ferguson, Graham 134
Filgate, Terry 179
Film Culture 140
Film Inquiry 7, 13, 45
Film Journalism 7
Les Fils de l'Eau 69, 70

Flaherty, Frances 34, 35, 38
Flaherty, Robert 6, 14, 18, 29, 32, 35, 36, 37, 38, 39,
    42, 62, 67, 72, 83, 84, 98, 109, 133
Fonda, Jane 89, 93
Football 97
Ford, Charles 9
Frank, Robert 141
Free Cinema 3, 7, 18, 42, 52-57, 62
Freund, Karl 68, 69
The Fun Couple 93

Gimbel, Roger 177
Gimme Shelter 125, 130, 131
The Glass House 177
Godard, Jean-Luc 7, 46, 48, 49, 140
Goldman, Lucien 5
Goodbye and Good Luck 134
Goodman, Benny 61
Goretta, Claude 54
Graham, Billy 61
Graham, Peter 6, 11, 79, 123, 127
Grassian, Dolores 183
Grierson, John 3, 37
Griffith, D. W. 68
Griffith, Richard 55

Haleff, Maxine 154
Happy Mother's Day (formerly called The Fischer Quintu-
    plets) 94, 95, 96, 181
Harris, Hillary 60
Heisenberg, Warner 37
Herman, Jean 123
Les Hommes de la Balaine 117
Horne, Denis 55, 56
Houston, Penelope 50
Humphrey, Hubert 87, 88
Hurwitz 37

Incident on Wilson Street 134, 137
Les Inconnus de la Terre (The Unknown of the Earth) 117,
    165, 183
The Investor and the Marketplace 177
Ivan the Terrible 9
Ivens, Joris 37

Jacobowski, Wanda 41
Jacobs, Lewis 56
Jaffe, Patricia 8, 16, 37, 95, 96, 152
Jane 89, 93
Je Suis la Président de la Républic 78
Jeanson 76
Jersey, William C., Jr. 7, 133, 134, 135, 137, 181
Le Jetée 122
Le Joli Mai (Pretty May) 15, 50, 123, 124, 165, 173, 183
Jones, Eugene S. 61
Julien, Claude 89

Kaufman, Denis Arkadievitch (actual name of Dziga Vertov) 23
Kaufman, Mikhail 27
Kelly, Ronald 17
Kennedy, Jacqueline 61
Kennedy, John F. 87, 88, 172
Kerouac, Jack 141
Kino-Eye 2, 25, 28, 30, 31
Kino-Nedelia 24
Kino-Pravda 6, 24, 25, 75, 115
Korda, Zolton 36
Kramer, Carl 58
Kudelski, Stefan 7, 181
Kuleshov 23

Labarthe, André 9
Lambert, Gavin 52
Lanoé, Henri 183
Larry 177
The Last Laugh 68
Lawson, John Howard 30
Leacock, Richard 6, 7, 8, 9, 12, 15, 16, 18, 27, 29, 73,
    83, 84, 85, 86, 87, 88, 89, 91, 92, 93, 94, 95, 96, 97,
    98, 99, 100, 101, 105, 106, 107, 108, 109, 118, 119,
    121, 123, 125, 131, 153, 163, 172, 179, 180, 181
Leslie, Alfred 141
Lettre de Sibérie 122
Levine, Joseph 125, 130
Lhomme, Pierre 15, 16, 118, 183
Lipscomb, James C. 4, 14, 124, 125
Living Camera 7, 29, 85, 88, 89, 91, 92, 93, 94, 97, 107
Look Back in Anger 56
Loren, Sophia 61, 125

Lorentz, Pare 37
Louisiana Story 36, 38, 84
Luft, Herbert 68
Lumière, Auguste 3
Lumière, Louis 3
The Lutheran Film Associates 181
Lyon Conference 7

MacFadden, Patrick 130, 131
McGowen, Tom 134
MacLeish, Archibald 60
Les Maitres Fous (The Manic Priests) 70
The Making of a President 89
Malakowski 26
Malle, Louis 47
A Man and a Woman 177
Man of Aran 35, 38, 39, 83
The Man with the Movie Camera 29, 38
Mandell, Hans 177
Manhattan Battleground 134, 135
Manvell, Roger 41, 42, 43, 49, 50
Marcorelles, Louis 7, 8, 15, 49, 77, 86, 92, 109, 127, 130
Marker, Chris 6, 15, 46, 50, 121, 122, 123, 124, 165, 172, 177, 183
May, Renato 5
Maysles, Albert 7, 29, 60, 86, 87, 90, 123, 124, 125, 127, 130, 131, 133, 153, 154, 165, 179, 180, 181
Maysles, David 7, 29, 60, 86, 87, 123, 124, 125, 127, 130, 131, 153, 154, 165, 181
Mazzetti, Lorenz 53
Mead, Margaret 176
Meet Marlon Brando 125
Mekas, Jonas 48, 93, 140, 141
Meppiel, Jacqueline 183
Meyers, Sidney 37
Moana 35, 36, 38, 39
Mobile Camera 7
Moi, un Noir (I, a Black) 71, 78, 140, 141, 173
Momma Don't Allow 53
Monterey Pop 176
Die Morder Sind Unter Uns (The Murderers Are Among Us) 42
Morillère, Roger 182, 183
Morin, Edgar 6, 7, 69, 72, 73, 155, 182
Motion Picture Academy 127
Murnau, F. W. 36

Nagra Tape Recorder 7
Nanook of the North 34, 35, 36, 39
National Broadcasting Company 61
National Film Board of Canada 74, 77, 154, 165
National Film Theatre 53
Nehru 93, 94, 106, 172, 180
Nehru, Jawaharlal 94, 97
Neo-realism 3, 4, 7, 18, 37, 41, 42, 43, 44, 45, 46, 47, 57, 62, 99
New Wave see Nouvelle Vague
Nice Time 54
Nouvelle Vague (New Wave) 3, 7, 18, 41, 46, 47, 48, 49, 50, 52, 57, 62, 115, 120, 121, 138, 140

O Dreamland 53
On the Bowery 139
Ossessione 41, 43
Other Voices 176

Paris Vu Par 77
Pennebaker, Donn Alan 86, 87, 88, 91, 125, 176, 179, 180, 181
Perraut, Michel 184
Personal Documentary 7
Pete and Johnnie 89
Petite Ville 118
Plebe, Armando 7, 91
Politique des auteurs 46
Ponti, Carlo 119, 184
Pour la Suite du Monde (For Posterity) 154, 162, 165, 173, 184
Presley, Elvis 47
Prévert 76
Primary 87, 88, 89, 93, 94, 125, 153, 154, 163, 172, 179
Prisoner at Large 134
Pudovkin, V. 10, 23
Pull My Daisy 141
La Punition (The Punishment) 73, 74, 76, 77, 182
La Pyramide Humaine 71, 72, 74

Les Quatre Cents Coup 48
The Queen 177
Quellet, Georges 181

Radio Television Française   7
Ravel, Jean   117, 182, 183
Realistic Cinema   7
Regard sur la Folie (A Look at Madness)   117, 183
Reichenbach   6, 123
Reisz, Karel   7, 52, 55, 56
Renoir, Jean   60, 100, 149
Rentrée de Classes   119
Resnais, Alain   47
Richardson, Tony   53, 56
Richter, Kenneth   158, 159
Richter Cine Equipment, Inc.   153
Robinson, David   56
Robinson, Edward G.   71
Rogosin, Lionel   138, 139
Rolling Stones   130, 131
Roma, Citta Aperta (Rome, Open City)   41, 42
Room at the Top   56
Rose et Landry   77
Rossellini, Roberto   7, 10, 41, 42, 76, 127
Rotha, Paul   27, 28, 30, 31, 36, 55
Rouch, Jean   6, 7, 8, 9, 11, 15, 18, 29, 37, 38, 46, 47,
    50, 67, 68, 69, 70, 71, 72, 73, 74, 75, 76, 77, 78, 79,
    80, 95, 101, 105, 106, 107, 108, 109, 115, 116, 117,
    118, 119, 121, 122, 123, 127, 140, 141, 155, 172, 182
Rozier, Jacques   50, 119, 120, 121, 184
Ruspoli, Mario   5, 7, 16, 18, 29, 46, 58, 79, 115, 116,
    117, 118, 119, 149, 153, 154, 156, 165, 179, 183
Ryden, Hope   125

Sadoul, Georges   6, 8, 24, 26, 28
Sagan, Françoise   47
Salesman   125, 130
Saturday Night and Sunday Morning   56
Sawyer, David   176
Sciuscia (Shoeshine)   41
The Search   42
Search into Darkness   134
Shadows   140
Shivas, Mark   120, 121
Showman   125, 127, 130, 163, 165, 173, 181
Shuker, Gregory   86, 91, 94, 125, 180, 181
Sillitoe, Alan   56
Simon, Frank   177
Sipherd, Ray   61
Smith, Hubert   10

Souto, Mario 157
Staudte, Wolfgang 42
Storey, David 56
Swallow, Norman 7, 62, 155
Synchronous Cinema 7

Tabu 36
Tanner, Alain 54, 70
Tarbes, Jean-Jacques 182
Tele-Vérité 7, 62
La Terre Treme (The Earth Trembles) 44
Tessier, Danielle 183
Thirard, Paul-Louis 108
This Sporting Life 56
A Time for Burning 134, 135, 137, 171, 181
Toby 85
Together 53, 54, 56
Tomorrow Entertainment 177
Truffaut, François 46, 47, 48, 177
Truth Film 7
Turksib 83
Two Women 125

Umberto D 43

Vadim, Roger 47
Van Doren, Mark 60
Van Dyke, Willard 11, 37, 134
Varda, Agnes 46
Variety 68, 69
Vassilier Brothers 23
Vertov, Dziga 4, 6, 9, 14, 18, 23, 24, 25, 26, 27, 28,
     29, 30, 31, 32, 37, 38, 39, 43, 56, 62, 72, 75, 86, 98,
     106, 115
Les Veuves de Quinze Ans 77
Visconti, Luchino 41, 43, 44

A War of Children 177
Warner Brothers 134
We Are the Lambeth Boys 55
What Is Happening? The Beatles in the U.S.A. 125
White, Theodore W. 89

Young, Colin   7

Zanuck, Darryl F.   61
Zavattini, Cesaro   7, 11, 13, 41, 44, 101
Zimmerman, Fred   42
Zora, Eva   183
Zwerin, Charlotte   130